Praise for *The Second Decision*

As an entrepreneur, Randy Nelson has s  own them, and sold them. He has experienced the s from rapid growth to significant slowdowns and ev tories and challenges in business, combined with hi fficer give him a wealth of knowledge and experier, Randy has willingly shared his experiences with other business owners in one on one and small group settings as a student, peer, and coach. In this environment, he has developed the talent of asking tough questions of himself and others. In this next phase of his career, he has dedicated his efforts to helping even more entrepreneurs on their journeys. This book distills Randy's knowledge in a straightforward, no-nonsense approach that will help any entrepreneurial leader.

GREG FERGUSON
Owner, Victory Contracting

I encourage you to use Randy's Entrepreneur Qual Card very objectively, which may mean letting others help you assess the answers. Far too often I observe that for many entrepreneurial leaders commitment means "I know I should", or "I really want to", or "I'm going to really try", that's not what will get the job done to become a Qualified Entrepreneur".

BILL BUXTON
Master Chair, Vistage International;
CEO Peer Group, 13 time Chair Excellence Award

The Second Decision is a must-read if that amazing purpose and drive of yours created your current business success - but you're a bit edgy and nervous about how to move forward from here. This book goes way beyond the usual "nice-in-theory" business advice and gives you actual hands-on, do-able strategies for building a strong company with a game plan for lasting success!

CHRISTINE KANE
CEO, Uplevel You

Reading Randy's book and completing his Qual Card will go a long way in assisting the entrepreneur with that all important second decision to **launch and leave or launch and lead**—and win!

After 30 years of naval service from ensign to flag officer, 10 years of senior executive corporate leadership experience and now 5 years in higher education, I passionately believe that *The Second Decision is a must read for entrepreneurs at all stages of the corporate life cycle, and for every potential senior level executive/leader. Why? Proper qualification and self-awareness are essential at any level, and in any organization. Randy's critical self-assessment, disciplined and "qualified" approach, founded on solid core values, will provide a huge assist for the leader with their vision, clarity, process, and accountability!*

R.E. "BENNY" SUGGS
Rear Admiral, US Navy (retired)
Associate Vice Chancellor, NC State University

I love this book and I will be giving copies to every business client I coach. It is well written, incredibly well researched and pulls no punches.

In Randy's words "this is not just another book in which veteran entrepreneurs drop pearls of wisdom; it's an actual program for improving corporate leaders, and this was inspired by my service in the Navy from 1983 to 1989".

To qualify for his title of Officer of the Deck of the James Madison Nuclear Submarine, Randy had to have a working knowledge of every aspect of running the ship.

Randy hits home with his message by studying like an apprentice in each department as he was required to do in his Navy training, to gain the requisite knowledge and understanding "that it takes to run finance, marketing, production, distribution or sales."

The book challenges you to look inside of yourself by answering tough questions throughout. As Randy clearly demonstrates, there is an exhilarating freedom that comes from disciplined thinking and systematic execution.

The end result is a clear path to grow in your role as a leader and entrepreneur.

RICH RUSSAKOFF
"Coach to the Best"; Author of *Make Banks Compete To Lend You Money*

So you decided to go into business for yourself. You have a great idea, product or service and you venture out on your own and before you know it you've got a real business...customers, employees, inventory, payables, receivables.... Now what? As The Second Decision so aptly points out, that was the easy part.

As Randy Nelson points out, what separates the professional entrepreneur from the business person is knowing what role you should play in your company. If your business is ever going to grow, you have to ask yourself a very difficult question... Are you the best person in your company to be the CEO/leader of your company or should you stay in sales, product development or another position and hire someone to lead? *In a very simple format, Randy has created the Entrepreneur Qual Card to help business owners answer this very difficult question.*

I first met Randy in 1999 at MIT's Birthing of Giants program and quickly realized that he has the unique ability to take the complex and break it down into simple to understand pieces. The Second Decision should be a must read for all entrepreneurs wanting to take themselves and their business to the next level.

SAM O'KRENT
CEO, O'Krent's Abbey Flooring Center

Every seasoned entrepreneur has made the Second Decision, whether consciously or otherwise. Through insights gained from his own entrepreneurial journeys, Randy outlines a disciplined approach to that decision-making process that will help set both the venture and the entrepreneur on a course for success. I highly recommend this book for any budding entrepreneur so that he or she can make the Second Decision consciously, rather than through expensive lessons learned in the School of Hard Knocks.

TOM MILLER
Executive Director, NC State Entrepreneurship Initiative; Senior Vice-Provost, NC State University

Great read for bootstrappers and VC-backed entrepreneurs alike. Every founder must decide what they want to do when they grow up. But whoever thought such a hard decision is best made right as your company starts to hit it big? Make the right decision and you'll turn your current rocket ship into a repeatable process that is more valuable than any single exit.

AARON W. HOUGHTON
Serial Entrepreneur; Co-founder at iContact.com; Co-founder and CEO at BoostSuite.com; #4 most influential CEO's under 30, Small business website Under30CEO, 2011

Randy Nelson's impact on our growing enterprise and me as its now qualified leader has been nothing short of remarkable. Our team has a newfound enthusiasm for accomplishing the vision Randy has helped us create with the assistance of his entrepreneurial qual card. After 30 years, we're acting like a real business!

SCOTT GRIFFIN
CEO, Practicon

There are a lot of business books written by some of the best. However, nothing beats what Randy has written about. It speaks to the essence of entrepreneurship, leadership and management. Through Randy's experiences he writes a masterpiece that every entrepreneur and CEO should read and re-read and then go out and follow his advice to maximize the value of your company.

JIM BAKER
CEO, Sumus Development Group, Inc.;
Co-Founder, Raleigh-Durham Chapter, Entrepreneurs Organization

The worst thing you can do as a leader is to not be self-aware of your shortcomings!

GREG LINDBERG
Eli Global, LLC

The academic study of business is one thing, real-world experience is another, and Randy has it in spades. This is a smart guy combining his financial background with his military discipline and the realities of what makes a successful business—sharing his wisdom and experience with us—Priceless.

PAUL LEVERING
Partner, BlueHat Mechanical

Successful CEOs are not born, they are made and developed. No matter if you are just starting out or consider yourself a seasoned entrepreneur we can all use help in developing a blue print on how to start and grow a profitable company. I have had the privilege of working with Randy for over 14 years and the tools listed in the Second Decision are the ones he has taught me over the years and the same ones I use to run and grow my business today.

DARRELL MCDANIEL
President, NSTAR Global Services

Randy Nelson has superbly encapsulated the essence of his military experience and his entrepreneurial experience into an invaluable tool for the leaders of post start-up companies—the "Entrepreneur Qual Card." As a subsequent leader of Orion, Randy's first start-up, I leaned heavily on his expertise and have found much success through the years as a result. Having all of his expertise in one book will serve as a very valuable resource for any entrepreneur facing the inherent challenges of leading and growing a successful business.

MIKE STARICH
Former U.S. Marine Corps officer; President, Orion International

If you have already beaten the odds and established a successful business, this book is a necessity. Randy's remarkable insights give you the clarity to define your optimal role in your business and unlock the highest possible value and enjoyment from your hard work.

JON JORDAN
CEO, Atlantic BT (6 time Inc. 5000 award winner)

I participate in a CEO advisory board with Randy Nelson: we've got Inc. 500 winners, guys that have sold 8-9 figure companies...some really sharp minds sitting around the table. That we (affectionately) nicknamed him "Yoda" tells you all you need to know. I've learned a lot from Randy while growing my business this year to #753 on the Inc. 5000 list, and so can every other business leader.

BRETT WATKINS
President, L&E Research

The Second Decision ...the QUALIFIED Entrepreneur... hits the nail on the head! ...addressing the unspoken truth that is needed to successfully make the transition from entrepreneur hyped-on-growth to a real CEO and leader focused on value creation.

KENNETH H. MARKS
Managing Partner, High Rock Partners;
Author of *The Handbook of Financing Growth*

Randy's unique and common sense approach to business has helped me take my businesses to a new level. I would recommend his teachings to any business owner who is serious about success.

GORDON JONES
CEO, Coldwell Banker Seaside Realty, Seaside Vacations

In the exciting, fast paced, and high flying world of entrepreneurship the world often overlooks one of its most important facets, the need for discipline. Randy does a great job of challenging founders to decide what type of entrepreneur they want to be and then shows them how to be one that manages their business with discipline.

CHRIS NG CASHIN
Co-founder, The Thundershirt Company

Every Entrepreneurial leader needs a well thought out game plan. I've been around a number of highly accomplished coaches & CEO's in my career and this is a must read!

ANTHONY DILWEG
Former NFL Quarterback; CEO, The Dilweg Companies

If you are willing to commit to the Entrepreneur Qual Card, Randy Nelson's "Second Decision" will generate an off the chart ROI. Randy has proven he knows how to lead during times of strong growth as well as the steep downturns we all cringe thinking about.

BILL MURPHY
CEO, Murphy, Inc.

I have been with Randy in his Vistage group for over 10 years, and I can sum it up very succinctly: The Second Decision is a must read for the entrepreneur who wants to build a sustainable company for the long term.

BRIAN ALLEN
CEO, Precision Walls

Randy is a seasoned serial entrepreneur, but more importantly a mentor to me and others. Many of us look up to him as Luke did to Yoda. I've learned plenty just in the questions he asks. I am forever grateful for his willingness to share his experiences in our EO forum. For you readers who are about to meet him, get ready to learn from one of the good guys!

KYLE BREISCHAFT
EO Member; CEO, Adaptive Health Systems, LLC

This book makes a fresh and highly valuable contribution to entrepreneurs everywhere. Successfully making the "Second Decision" is what separates highly successful business leaders from perpetually struggling entrepreneur wannabes. After all, in today's world of pop-up online businesses and start-ups de jour, opening a new business isn't the hardest part...staying in business and profitably growing over the long term is the real trick. This is where Randy's depth of experience really pays off for readers. Rooted in real-world experiences from his highly-successful military and business endeavors, Randy shows us the importance of becoming qualified business owners and leaders. Importantly, he also guides us through the process of finding our best and most authentic role that will contribute the most towards the ultimate success of the business: the leader, role-player or creator. So, pick up this book, settle in at your favorite coffee shop, and start your journey to becoming a qualified entre-

preneur. Your business, your employees, your investors, your family...and most importantly, your customers...will thank you for it.

DAVID W. WILSON
CEO, FGI Research & Analytics; Founder, Alliance Medical Ministry

I have had the pleasure of participating with Randy in a Vistage Group for the past 7 years. Randy's insights into both personal and business level accountability have consistently had a direct impact on our company's performance.

MARK LEE
President, Baker Roofing

Very few athletes truly want the ball in their hands at the end of the game and are capable of delivering the winning shot consistently. Randy is that guy...somebody you don't want to be playing on the final nine in match play on a golf course...he brings the same mentality to building successful businesses and wants to see the future success of the organization in the hands of a qualified entrepreneur...don't read this book unless you want and can handle that responsibility as the leader!

DENNIS KELLEY/ALEX CHANDLER/MARK BOUMENOT/PETE ZSOLDOS
Glen Laurel Partners

THE
SECOND
DECISION

THE DECISION SERIES FOR ENTREPRENEURS™

THE
SECOND
DECISION

the QUALIFIED entrepreneur™

RANDY H. NELSON

Foreword by **General Hugh Shelton**, 14th Chairman, Joint Chiefs of Staff

Published by Advantage, Charleston, South Carolina.
Member of Advantage Media Group.

ADVANTAGE is a registered trademark and the Advantage colophon is a trademark of Advantage Media Group, Inc.

Printed in the United States of America.

ISBN: 978-1-59932-545-3
LCCN: 2014957788

Book design by Megan Elger.

This publication is designed to provide accurate and authoritative information in regard to the subject matter covered. It is sold with the understanding that the publisher is not engaged in rendering legal, accounting, or other professional services. If legal advice or other expert assistance is required, the services of a competent professional person should be sought.

Advantage Media Group is proud to be a part of the Tree Neutral® program. Tree Neutral offsets the number of trees consumed in the production and printing of this book by taking proactive steps such as planting trees in direct proportion to the number of trees used to print books. To learn more about Tree Neutral, please visit www.treeneutral.com. To learn more about Advantage's commitment to being a responsible steward of the environment, please visit www.advantagefamily.com/green

Advantage Media Group is a publisher of business, self-improvement, and professional development books and online learning. We help entrepreneurs, business leaders, and professionals share their Stories, Passion, and Knowledge to help others Learn & Grow. Do you have a manuscript or book idea that you would like us to consider for publishing? Please visit advantagefamily.com or call 1.866.775.1696.

Dedicated to Kristi and Mom,
the two women who have loved and guided me throughout my life,
I am forever grateful.

CONTENTS

xix | **FOREWORD**
The *Qualified* Entrepreneur

1 | **CHAPTER 1**
What Is the Second Decision?

19 | **CHAPTER 2**
The Challenge of Startup Success

31 | **CHAPTER 3**
Start by Stopping...and Slow Down to Speed Up!

43 | **CHAPTER 4**
What Kind of Leader Are You?

59 | **CHAPTER 5**
How To Develop and Brief Your Three-Year Vision

79 | **CHAPTER 6**
Execution: Goals and Accountability
and Key Leadership Decision #1

93 | **CHAPTER 7**
Six Months' Cash and Covenants
and Key Leadership Decision #2

115 | **CHAPTER 8**
COGS-nizance: Profit and Expense Leadership

135 | **CHAPTER 9**
Metrics: Mining for Gold

153 | **CHAPTER 10**
Values-Based Leadership

167 | **CHAPTER 11**
Career-Long Learning

187 | **CHAPTER 12**
Bor-E-Gaged

203 | **CHAPTER 13**
Crisis Leadership, Contingency Planning and the
RESET Button

227 | **CHAPTER 14**
Reflection: Peer Advice and Insights

247 | **CHAPTER 15**
The Second Decision

271 | **APPENDIX A**
An Excerpt from *The Third Decision*

281 | **APPENDIX B**
The Entrepreneur Qual Card

299 | **APPENDIX C**
The Seawater Question Answered!

303 | **APPENDIX D**
Line Officer Submarine Qual Card (Excerpt)

307 | **NOTES**

317 | **THANK YOU'S**

THE QUALIFIED ENTREPRENEUR

by General H. Hugh Shelton (Ret.)

I was honored to serve as Chairman of the Joint Chiefs of Staff (1997–2001) where I was the principal military advisor to two different presidents, Bill Clinton and George W. Bush. Since my retirement in 2001, I have had the opportunity to serve on and chair several corporate boards, both in the private and public sectors. That has provided me the opportunity to observe numerous leaders over the past 40-plus years, in many different capacities.

As I retired from the US Army, I discovered that I wanted to give back to the community in which my wife and I grew up. So I was delighted when I was approached by my *alma mater*, NC State University, and offered the opportunity to create the General H. Hugh Shelton Leadership Center. The mission of the center is to inspire, educate, and develop values-based leaders committed to personal integrity, professional ethics, and selfless service. To ensure the success of the center, we formed a Leadership Advisory Board and filled it with some of the best leaders I had known throughout my career in the military, along with others from the community, state, and nation who volunteered to be part of this leadership initiative.

This is where I first met Randy Nelson.

From the beginning, it was obvious that Randy's insights and contributions to the advisory board were having a significant impact on the Center. At that time, Randy was serving as the president of Orion International, a company that transitions military personnel into full-time civilian work. To date, Orion has placed over 25,000 exiting service men and women into post-military careers, and the company continues to lead the nation in this market.

Randy joined the leadership board because he had a passion for both values-based leadership and giving back to the community. During more than six years as a US Navy lieutenant in the US Nuclear Submarine force, Randy developed his own extraordinary leadership skills, which he then applied as he built his own businesses (Orion International and NSTAR Global Services) beginning in 1991.

What I immediately observed about Randy was that he brought a number of different perspectives to the table. The creative, entrepreneurial ideas that have made him so successful in his business career, along with the seasoned leadership that grew from his time in the US Navy, were invaluable in making our own startup, the Shelton Leadership Center, a reality. Randy shared his own experiences as they related to the various challenges we faced as we built the Center, and his willingness to share both the mistakes and successes of his career was invaluable.

Randy has a very professional demeanor and his leadership skills were immediately evident to the rest of the Leadership Advisory Board at the Shelton Leadership Center. He consistently demonstrates a unique blend of creativity acquired through his entrepreneurial education and experience, and a professional discipline of the type required to build successful companies like Orion and NSTAR. The sustained growth of the Shelton Leadership Center is due, in no small way, to Randy's advice, experience, and commitment.

Having led and been led in all segments of society over the past 40-plus years, I understand that I must earn the respect of my peers, superiors, and subordinates—and all the truly great leaders I have observed understand the same. Randy has earned our board's ultimate respect, as demonstrated by the fact that he has been selected as chairman of our board of advisors. He will be the first person to let you know that his selection is only the beginning of the hard work, and that he will need to continue to earn respect in the future. But I would expect nothing less.

The Second Decision lets the reader into Randy's world, where he combines his entrepreneurial instincts with his regimen of discipline to create an entrepreneur qualification system for those who have the desire to learn and develop their own leadership skills. Having witnessed his impact with the Leadership Center at NC State, I am confident that this book and its unique approach to career-long education and improvement for entrepreneurs will have a very significant impact on the companies and careers of those who read Randy's book. Randy has walked in your shoes, and he is willing to share the lessons he has learned, even the hard ones, for the benefit of your own career as a leader.

Whether you are a lifelong learner who wants to continually improve, like me and Randy, or an entrepreneur with a desire to enhance your own discipline—or maybe even a military or other type of leader with plenty of discipline but seeking more entrepreneurial skills—this book is for you. I say this assuming, of course, that you are willing to look in the mirror and hold yourself accountable firstly and ahead of all others. That is what great leaders do, and that is what a *Qualified* Entrepreneur *must* do to lift his or her organization to its maximum potential. So strap in; this self-awareness journey is going to be challenging, it's going to require dedication, and you will need to truly commit to your own improvement as a leader. The results you achieve will be worth it—but you already know this, or you wouldn't have picked up this book!

WHAT IS THE SECOND DECISION?

"Success is peace of mind, which is a direct result of self-satisfaction in knowing you did your best to become the best you are capable of becoming"

—JOHN R. WOODEN

The First Decision was made on the day that you started your company. That was when the dream was made real. An entrepreneur was born, a company was established, and the work began.

It took guts and endless hours to get your business to the success it enjoys today, and now you're at the helm of an organization that is growing in numbers of employees and, potentially, in layers of management. Day-to-day issues are becoming more complex. Growth is either out of control or hard to maintain. And out there in the near or distant future awaits maturity, with its own set of challenges.

The books written about making the First Decision—to start an entrepreneurial company—can fill small libraries. But until now there hasn't been a book squarely aimed at the Second Decision™.

What is it? The Second Decision is the choice you make when you fully realize the responsibility that rests on your shoulders. Are you enjoying this? Are you up to the task? Most importantly: **Do you possess the vision, the personal skills, the perseverance, and the nuts-and-bolts knowledge that your company needs from its leader at this stage of its growth?** If not, can you get there? Do you want to? The Second Decision is about whether or not to become a *Qualified* Entrepreneur™!

You may know the answers to some of those questions already, or think you do. But this book offers you the opportunity to take a self-awareness journey in search of the real data you'll need for making a well-reasoned Second Decision. It invites you to really explore how ready you are for continued and expanded leadership and, with that, whether you're ready to take the steps necessary to become what I call a *Qualified* Entrepreneur.

So as we begin, let's define your first step towards becoming a *Qualified* Entrepreneur: your graduation from entrepreneur to the *Disciplined* Entrepreneur™, which is an entrepreneur who:

- … becomes fully self-aware that *they don't know what they don't know*, and that it's better to achieve a status of "*I know what I don't know.*" This self-knowledge makes it clear how the entrepreneur's shortcomings may be affecting his/her company…and usually results in a commitment to a lifelong learning process.

- … becomes fully self-aware that, for the business to succeed long term, a transition must occur from the business being about "me" as its entrepreneur/CEO to being about the overall needs of the company.

- … commits to undertaking the preparation necessary for making the Second Decision. This is a conscious choice to acquire a more disciplined approach to management and leadership—or to bring that discipline to the company in another way. The *Disciplined* Entrepreneur knows that it's less important how his/her role is shaped than that the company excels and succeeds.

Revealing my bias right here and now, I hope that becoming a *Qualified* Entrepreneur ends up being your Second Decision. As part of this decision, you could opt to remain the leader. You could decide to share some of your leadership responsibilities with someone who brings skills that you lack. You could choose to move on and start another company too, if that's what's best for you and your current business. There are other possible outcomes as well. Whatever the result, I know that becoming more aware of your strengths and weaknesses is a desirable goal for an entrepreneur or CEO. I know this because I've seen its value in my own life and career.

And I am not alone, by a long shot. Berkshire Hathaway vice-chairman Charles T. Munger, when asked how the company that he and Warren Buffett built shot past GE in market value, responded by saying, "I think Warren and I have had a temperamental advantage: Warren and I know better than most people what we know and what we don't know. That's even better than having a lot of extra IQ points."[1] In a June 2012 *Inc.* magazine article titled "Be Great Now," noted author Jim Collins stated, "The great leaders I have studied are all people whose energy and drive are directed outward. It's not about themselves. It's about something greater than themselves."

The Second Decision journey towards becoming the *Qualified* Entrepreneur will be about both leadership and entrepreneurship, starting with your commitment to embrace the definition of a *Disciplined* Entrepreneur!

HOW I BECAME A *QUALIFIED* ENTREPRENEUR

I have been both an entrepreneur and a CEO. I started my first fast-growth company (with partners) in 1991. Based near Raleigh-Durham, NC, where I live, Orion International has placed more than 25,000 exiting military personnel in industry jobs. This makes it the largest military recruiting company in the United States. I don't own Orion anymore, having sold it to private equity investors in 2007, but I continue to assist its leaders by remaining on the board of directors. In 2002, I founded NSTAR Global Services, a services and staffing provider in the semiconductor industry. I'm proud to say that NSTAR was named to the *Inc.* 500/5000 for four consecutive years, ranking no. 163 in 2007. When it was sold in 2010 to a German conglomerate, M+W Group, I stayed on with the parent for just shy of four years, developing NSTAR's global presence.

In 2012 I began the work that led to this book. Looking back over two decades of founding companies, building them, and sustaining their growth through two significant recessions, I felt proud of my accomplishments. But I also felt amazed and plenty relieved: amazed that I had managed to muddle through all the ups and downs, despite really knowing very little about how to run a business, and relieved—more relieved than I can accurately convey—to have come out the other side with two thriving companies on my résumé. Through networking with other entrepreneurs and CEOs regarding their experiences and comparing them to mine, I realized that we all had something important we could provide to the entrepreneurs who follow us: the benefit of our own experience and the school-of-hard-knocks education it provided us.

But this is not just another book in which veteran entrepreneurs drop pearls of wisdom; it's an actual program for improving corporate leaders, and this was inspired by my service in the US Navy from 1983 to 1989.

Being in the military showed me what we lack when we become entrepreneurs or when we morph from entrepreneur to CEO: *a means of knowing whether we're up to the job.* Knowing who's qualified has never been a problem in the US Navy—or in any branch of the military, for that matter. When you're in the service, you can just look at somebody's uniform and know what they've been doing and, more importantly, what they know. You don't really see the person, not at first. You see the uniform. You see the decorations that signify time, training, and skills developed—and *then* you see the person.

Picture me in 1987, at age 25. Any civilian who spotted me in street clothes would figure me to be a kid just out of college and, given my conservative haircut, maybe new to the job market. But, with my uniform on, its decorations tell another story: I'm a lieutenant for the US Navy, and I make my living driving the USS *James Madison*, 425 feet of nuclear-powered steel submarine. I have achieved the title of Officer of the Deck, which means that I'm qualified to be in charge of the entire ship and its crew. On any starry night back in that era, you might have found me at the helm, standing a six-hour watch every 18 hours of our time at sea.

I cannot tell you how much I loved that job. Watching dolphins nose the bow after we had surfaced from the deep (where a sub spends 99 percent of the time) never, ever got old. It was a thrill every time, and I still feel it when I recall it, even 25 years later. It was a thrill of a different and greater kind, though, to be leading the highly trained staff that monitored the many computerized mechanical and electrical systems of the ship. It was one of the great honors of my life to be one of just a handful of men charged with carrying out the captain's orders as he slept, thus ensuring the other 14 officers and 132 crewmen a good night's sleep as well.

> At each point in the US Navy's regimented process I was vying for the *gold dolphins pin* on my uniform, reflecting not just completion or credentialing, but excellence. It was hard work, and work that was truly worthy.

Part of my pride and pleasure, both then and later, came from knowing that I *earned* this position of extreme responsibility, piece by piece, through training, testing, and more training and testing. At each point in the US Navy's regimented process I was vying for the *gold dolphins pin* on my uniform, reflecting not just completion or credentialing, but excellence. It was hard work, and work that was truly worthy. (The gold dolphins pin is the submariner's version of pilot wings.)

In the decades that have passed since I left the US Navy to build and sell businesses, I've often asked myself two questions:

1. If I couldn't stand watch on a nuclear submarine without undergoing the necessary discipline to become qualified, certified, and ready . . . then **what on earth made me think I could establish, build, and successfully lead a company to maturity just because I wanted to?**

2. **What if entrepreneurial and fast-growth businesses required of their leaders a submarine-like set of qualifications?** Indeed, what if entrepreneurial CEOs like me had to clear the requirements of a US Navy-like "Qual Card" to earn the equivalent of a gold dolphin at each level of growth and responsibility?

My own experiences in business fed this line of thinking. As much as I felt prepared for military leadership by the US Navy, I felt *un*prepared for most of the civilian responsibilities I shouldered in the first decade of my business career. Hard times in my businesses made me increasingly hard on myself, and deservedly so. Looking back, I can clearly see that I didn't know much of what I needed to know. Worse, for a long time *I didn't know what I didn't know.*

"I am a drop of seawater about to enter the submarine. Explain how I turn the light on over your bed when you're done with your work and want to read a book."

The above question was one I had to answer to the captain's satisfaction if I wanted to earn my gold dolphins and win the right to drive his submarine. It was an ingenious question, because to answer it I had to completely understand the submarine. I had to have at least a general command of the working of every system on the ship and—more importantly—a grasp of how the various systems combine to contribute to the good of the whole.

Are you wondering how I answered the question? I'll talk about that later, when the answer becomes most relevant to your efforts to become a *Qualified* Entrepreneur. No peeking!

Running a business is a lot like trying to answer the seawater question. As an entrepreneur or CEO, you don't need to understand every detail of every function in the operation. But you do need to know why each function exists, what it does, and how it contributes to the overall success of the enterprise.

It's my experience that most of us entrepreneurs and CEOs think we have a better handle on the levers that drive our businesses than we actually do. I know, because I was one of the ones who erroneously claimed mastery. I now know that, without having studied or apprenticed in each division or department, neither I nor any entrepreneurial leader can claim more than a basic understanding of what it takes to run Finance, Marketing, Production, Distribution, or Sales. That's just the truth of the matter.

Ideally, of course, we entrepreneurs and CEOs would be more knowledgeable than everybody we manage. That's rare, though. The rest of us—and we are legion—would benefit from a better understanding of the vast reaches of what we don't know, and a dose of the humility that goes with it.

The Small Business Administration's figures on business failure are sobering: 50 percent of new companies are gone 5 years out, and nearly 70 percent are history at 10 years (throughout the remainder of the book I will use 70 percent as the failure rate—historical statistics range from 66.7 to 70 percent).[2, 3] What's equally disturbing to me, though, are the many companies that simply underproduce. They may last a long time, but they never achieve what they could—and if management or leadership issues aren't the entire cause of the problem, they are certainly a factor.

I firmly believe that this book's program of leadership and managerial self-assessment will help to reduce the failure rate of entrepreneurial companies in this nation. It should also increase the longevity and productivity of companies that are reaching the often-dangerous phases of their lives—fast growth, becoming fully managed, and ultimately reaching maturity.

Borrowing from the US Navy's "Qual Card" certification system, in this book I have established a "Qual Card" process of my own. In essence, I've created an entrepreneur's own certification system—a means by which entrepreneurs and entrepreneurial CEOs can develop skills and be ready for the demands of leading the larger, more complex companies that begin growing immediately post-startup. When you "graduate" from my program, you'll be a *Qualified* Entrepreneur. You can see excerpts from my original US Navy Qual Card in Appendix D. (Thanks to the US Navy for giving me permission to put this into *The Second Decision*!)

In each chapter we'll consider an aspect of entrepreneurial/ corporate leadership, detailing what's required of the person at the helm. At the end of each chapter, you'll have the opportunity to conduct a performance review on yourself, essentially asking, "Do I have the skills I need?" With these self-assessments in place, you'll reach the end of the book able to evaluate how well you're equipped to "complete the mission"—for your employees, your investors, and advisers, but most importantly, for your own satisfaction and fulfillment. You'll have made the Second Decision.

Ram Charan, an author and adviser to top global business leaders, challenges us all to *double our personal capacity every three years.*[4] When I heard him speak to a large group of entrepreneurs recently, I knew his message had special relevance in the context of this book. Charan points out that, when it comes to your personal capacity, maintaining the status quo is, in reality, a step backwards. You're losing ground to your competition whenever you're standing still, he says. Undergoing the process necessary to become a *Qualified* Entrepreneur is definitely a step toward increasing your own personal capacity for successful entrepreneurship . . . and long-term leadership. It also is just the beginning of your commitment to improving *You, Inc.* The Qual Card process in *The Second Decision* is just the starting gate!

> It also is just the beginning of your commitment to improving *You, Inc.* The Qual Card process in *The Second Decision* is just the starting gate!

Throughout this book, you'll learn more about my successes and failures as an entrepreneur and CEO, as well as those of my peers. What I've learned forms the backbone of the material I present, chapter by chapter. But this is *your self-awareness journey.* This is *your* invitation to become a *Qualified* Entrepreneur. Experience in starting and building companies has led me to believe that being led by a *Qualified* Entrepreneur is what's best for growing companies and the people who populate them. Still, it's only best for the company when it's also best for the person at the top. Trouble starts when there's a mismatch between your skills and interests, and the needs of the company.

KNOW YOUR ROLE OR ROLES

As a CEO and entrepreneur, you likely wear one of about seven hats—and maybe more than one at a time! Here are the different titles or roles of business leadership. Think about which hats you wear.

Founder/Entrepreneur: An individual who organizes and operates a business or businesses, taking on financial risk to do so.

Accidental Entrepreneur: Sometimes ideas are pursued and companies are formed more from circumstances than an actual plan. In my eyes, you're an accidental entrepreneur if you did not actively seek the role of the entrepreneur—instead, it sought you!

Partner: One that is united or associated with another or others in an activity or a sphere of common interest, especially a member of a business partnership.

President: A leader of an organization or company (or club, trade union, institution, nation, or just about anything else that one might preside over).

Chief Operating Officer (COO): The holder of this title is one of the highest-ranking executives in an organization, comprising part of the "C-suite." The COO is responsible for the daily operation of the company and routinely reports to the highest ranking executive, who is usually the Chief Executive Officer.

Chief Executive Officer (CEO): The highest-ranking corporate officer (executive) or administrator in charge of the total management of an organization. Sometimes the term is used interchangeably with president; sometimes there is one but not the other; sometimes an organization will employ both.

Of course, if I wanted to cover the full spectrum of modern leadership, I'd have to add a host of more creative titles. A *Forbes* columnist named "Princess of Possibility" the best title of 2012. It was the title then held by Min Xuan Lee, cofounder of a financial literacy website for kids called PlayMoolah.[5] "Sherpas" have proliferated lately—in fact, the top job in at least one company is "Strategy Sherpa."[6] CEOs are also calling themselves CIOs with increasing regularity, though they don't mean Chief Information Officer. Chief *Imagination* Officer is the president's title at New Holland Brewing Co.,[7] in Holland, Michigan, and I've also seen it mean Chief *Inspiration* Officer.[8] It gets even cuter. Business cards today may say "Head Cheese" for the CEO of, yes, a cheese company; the CEO of Honest Tea, Inc. is the TeaEO.[9] Farmer-owned Organic Valley hasn't got a CEO, it's got a "C-E-I-E-I-O."[10] Perhaps the reasoning behind all the creative naming is best expressed by one of the corporate perpetrators, a craft brewer: "Rogue is not a business, Rogue is a revolution. And revolutions don't have conventional titles," says Brett Joyce, whose preferred title is not President, but "Player Coach."[11]

So, let's leave aside the actual title on your business card. We should disregard the kind of company or industry you're in, too.

Yours may be a fast-growing startup, a family-owned business, a professional firm, or a rapidly maturing organization with at least part of a C-suite in place. What you have in common with others who read this book is that each of you is leading or helping to lead a successful organization, one that survived the First Decision—which was the decision to start your company. For the purposes of clarity, I will refer to you mostly as the entrepreneur or CEO, and we will talk about our varied types of businesses as ones that have a lot in common, because they do.

It's also important for each of you to take into consideration where you are on the life cycle of your organization when deciding upon your Second Decision. It may be a different choice if you are in a wildly successful growth phase or coming out of a challenging recession over the past few years. The "Greiner Curve," developed by Larry Greiner in the 1970s, describes phases that organizations go through as they grow.[12]

ACCORDING TO THE RECENT MINDTOOLS ARTICLE "THE GREINER CURVE":

All kinds of organizations—from design shops to manufacturers, construction companies to professional service firms—experience these. Each growth phase is made up of a period of relatively stable growth, followed by a "crisis" when major organizational change is needed if the company is to continue growing. Picture the phase that your organization is in, and use that position to guide you in your self-assessment moving forward. The Greiner Curve allows you to see what is coming next for you as its leader, but realize that each company may go through the stages differently.

PHASE 1: GROWTH THROUGH CREATIVITY

Here, the entrepreneurs who founded the firm are busy creating products and opening up markets. There aren't many staff, so informal communication works fine, and rewards for long hours are probably through profit share or stock options. However, as more staff join, production expands and capital is injected, there's a need for more formal communication.

*This phase ends with a **Leadership Crisis**, where professional management is needed. The founders may change their style and take on this role, but often someone new will be brought in.*

PHASE 2: GROWTH THROUGH DIRECTION

Growth continues in an environment of more formal communications, budgets and focus on separate activities like marketing and production. Incentive schemes replace stock as a financial reward.

However, there comes a point when the products and processes become so numerous that there are not enough hours in the day for one person to manage them all, and he or she can't possibly know as much about all these products or services as those lower down the hierarchy.

*This phase ends with an **Autonomy Crisis:** New structures based on delegation are called for.*

PHASE 3: GROWTH THROUGH DELEGATION

With mid-level managers freed up to react fast to opportunities for new products or in new markets, the organization continues to grow, with top management just monitoring and dealing with the big issues (perhaps starting to look at merger or acquisition opportunities). Many businesses flounder at this stage, as the manager whose directive approach solved the problems at the end of Phase 1 finds it hard to let go, yet the mid-level managers struggle with their new roles as leaders.

*This phase ends with a **Control Crisis:** A much more sophisticated head office function is required, and the separate parts of the business need to work together.*

PHASE 4: GROWTH THROUGH COORDINATION AND MONITORING

Growth continues with the previously isolated business units re-organized into product groups or service practices. Investment finance is allocated centrally and managed according to Return on Investment (ROI) and not just profits. Incentives are shared through company-wide profit share schemes aligned to corporate goals. Eventually, though, work becomes submerged under increasing amounts of bureaucracy, and growth may become stifled.

*This phase ends on a **Red-Tape Crisis:** A new culture and structure must be introduced.*

PHASE 5: GROWTH THROUGH COLLABORATION

The formal controls of phases 2-4 are replaced by professional good sense as staff group and re-group flexibly in teams to deliver projects in a matrix structure supported by sophisticated information systems and team-based financial rewards.

*This phase ends with a crisis of **Internal Growth:** Further growth can only come by developing partnerships with complementary organizations.*

PHASE 6: GROWTH THROUGH EXTRA-ORGANIZATIONAL SOLUTIONS

Greiner's recently added sixth phase suggests that growth may continue through merger, outsourcing, networks and other solutions involving other companies.

Growth rates will vary between and even within phases. The duration of each phase depends almost totally on the rate of growth of the market in which the organization operates. The longer a phase lasts, though, the harder it will be to implement a transition.

In his book *Scaling Up,* Verne Harnish defines 96 percent of businesses as "mice." Only 4 percent manage to grow up and achieve revenues over $1 million, and less than half of a percent manage to scale up beyond $10 million, with even fewer scaling to $50 million and beyond. As you start your self-awareness journey, you now have a good idea where you stand compared to the other entrepreneurs reading this book, both in terms of size and life cycle.

By the end of this book, you'll have all the information you need to ask and answer the big questions: Are you a *Qualified* Entrepreneur or on your way to becoming one? In that capacity, will you continue to **lead** your company, enhancing your company's future as you build your own skill set? Will you, instead, use the knowledge of a *Qualified* Entrepreneur to **support** your current company by taking on an internal role better suited to your skill set? Or will you take your improved skills and greater self-awareness out to the market, where you can once again **create** a new enterprise? There are no right answers. There is only self-evaluation, from which come choices. It is, indeed, a journey.

Your Second Decision is only chapters away. Welcome to the journey of the *Qualified* Entrepreneur.

CHAPTER 1 QUAL CARD

Initial each requirement as met:

PREREQUISITES	INITIALS
The entrepreneur fully understands and embraces the definition of the *Disciplined Entrepreneur* as outlined in this chapter.	_____
The entrepreneur understands and commits to the Qual Card process of self-evaluation presented in the book.	_____
The entrepreneur takes note of the growth phase his/her organization is at on the Greiner Curve and the key leadership decisions that he/she will face in the future.	_____
Inspired by Ram Charan's challenge, the entrepreneur commits to the work necessary to increase his/her personal capacity every two to three years.[13]	_____

SIGNATURE: _____

DATE: _____

CHAPTER 2

THE CHALLENGE OF STARTUP SUCCESS

"In reading the lives of great men [and women], I found that the first victory was over themselves... self-discipline with all of them came first."

—HARRY S. TRUMAN

What was it that made you pick up this book? Although I am the book's author, I am not the one presenting you with the Second Decision, and I am not the one asking you to consider becoming a *Qualified* Entrepreneur. Your company, your employees, and you yourself are the ones inviting you to consider your skills and capabilities—and you've picked up this book for the purpose of doing just that. In other words, you have created your own wonderful problem. Your company is no longer just an idea on a napkin. It has passed the startup test, it has shown its growth potential, and your employees need leadership, vision, and consistent execution to maintain and increase the business's success. I'll bet you've found yourself looking in the mirror and asking the same questions this book asks: At this point in the company's life, are you the right person for the job? Do you have what your company needs right now? What skills might you lack?

Let's just recognize the elephant in the room. Just as there's a bell curve reflecting the success of entrepreneurial startups, there's also a bell curve for growth companies. Is the entrepreneur or founder who succeeded so wildly in the startup phase similarly equipped to succeed in the growth phase and beyond to maturity? Some are, some aren't, and a whole host of them *can become so equipped*—but only if they want to. You've already proven your entrepreneurial skills and instincts. Not every entrepreneur wants to be CEO or wants to take the steps necessary to excel in that role. Anyone who is clear as to which side of the fence they prefer to live on—the entrepreneur's side or the CEO's—may not be reading this book. They're busy disentangling themselves from one startup so they can launch another . . . or they've happily beaten the curve and are excelling at all aspects of leading a company to maturity.

> Is the entrepreneur or founder who succeeded so wildly in the startup phase similarly equipped to succeed in the growth phase and beyond to maturity?

This book is for the rest of us, the ones for whom the answer maybe isn't as clear. Me? I'm the dyed-in-the-wool entrepreneur who gradually, sometimes painfully, learned how to become the *Qualified* Entrepreneur that I now know I was destined to be. This book aims to help you evaluate your skills and interests from the comfort of an easy chair, instead of in the trenches, hip-deep in mud, and possibly taking hostile fire.

DANGER AHEAD!

Over the course of my involvement in multiple startup companies and my coaching and consulting activities of recent years, I have identified four issues that prevent entrepreneurs from becoming *Qualified* Entrepreneurs even before they start. Watch out for them:

Insistence on autonomy. An *Inc.* magazine study a while back revealed that, regardless of age, gender, or the size or age of their companies, the one single factor that drives most entrepreneurs is their desire or need for autonomy.[1] And, as you can imagine, it's not something they (we) give up easily. In the startup phase, the company is all about you, the entrepreneur or founder. Your fingerprints are on everything, and there is very little you don't know and aren't directing. But when you clear the startup phase and enter the growth phase, your employee base and fixed costs grow, and the business almost certainly begins to experience some ups and downs. The bigger the company gets, the more complex the business becomes, and the more vulnerable it is to industry and macroeconomic trends. Those who maintain a stranglehold on their autonomy as entrepreneur or founder are likely to hinder the company's ability to respond quickly and intelligently to the many threats it faces. In the growth phase, you simply can't do it all, and it's foolish to keep believing you can.

Unwillingness to build structure, cultivate expertise, or delegate. Even those who recognize that they can't do it all—not beyond a certain level of growth, anyway—will sometimes have trouble with this one. When making the jump from entrepreneur to *Qualified* Entrepreneur, the plain fact is that many of us will need to surround ourselves with a strong executive team—or at least a steady right-hand individual—to ensure the company's long-term success. As you'll see, this book explores two aspects of discipline: the kind you need within yourself to move your organization forward, and the kind that produces good leadership decisions within a managerial team. To a large extent, the second kind of discipline results from structure of a type that entrepreneurs are often slow to create.

> Isn't it ironic that we entrepreneurs are so good at holding other people accountable as we grow, and demanding great performance from them to help us grow, yet *we don't do performance reviews on ourselves?*

As you grow your company and enlarge it to meet new opportunities, you must also build in accountability. Systems need to be put into place, and people, too. Part of the task is conducting performance reviews to know who your "A," "B," and "C" players are, and where their strongest skills lie. But who conducts a performance review on you? Isn't it ironic that we entrepreneurs are so good at holding other people accountable as we grow, and demanding great performance from them to help us grow, yet *we don't do performance reviews on ourselves?* Being so protective of our autonomy, we would probably fight such a review if someone were to propose it, right? That's why this book proposes that *you* make the decision to evaluate your own skills. Commit to becoming a *Qualified* Entrepreneur and you will find that you can keep much of your autonomy, and at the same time build (or watch selected others build) a successful organization that allows the company to reach its true potential. Choose to remain an entrepreneur who retains autonomy and doesn't instill discipline as a foundation for growth, however, and your organization will underachieve.

Boredom. A typical worker who grows bored with a job either takes a different job or becomes less productive in the current job. When boredom takes over in an entrepreneur, however, look out! Things are going to get up-ended in a hurry, because many bored entrepreneurs either start new companies or abruptly make changes in their current companies to keep their own level of excitement high. This one I know from experience. You come out of the exhilaration and total immersion of the startup experience, you savor some success, but then you fairly quickly start thinking about new conquests. Because your self-confidence is sky-high from what you've been able to do with a first company, you have little reservation about launching a second . . . or a third.

Of course, entrepreneurs are to be celebrated for their guts and desire to innovate. The world needs what we do! But when a serial entrepreneur habitually and almost obsessively looks for new sandboxes to play in, what happens to the existing company or companies often isn't very good. So, if you're one who is currently more bored than engaged (a variable state that I label as being "bor-e-gaged"), I'd like to ask you to put your entrepreneurial urges on hold at least long enough to read this book. It may sound a little lofty, but I really think this book can contribute to a reduction in that 70 percent 10-year failure rate in entrepreneurial companies.[2, 3]

And here, at last, is the last of what we might call the Four Horsemen of the (Entrepreneurial) Apocalypse:

Failure to engage in self-examination. How aware are you of your own strengths and weaknesses? This book will require you to set aside your probably abundant entrepreneurial self-confidence and take stock of what you know, what you're good at, and what skills you have yet to master in your leadership role. Remember, it's a "self-awareness journey." What each of us has to face at some point in our career is that great ideas well-executed don't automatically add up to a company that's "built to last," as author Jim Collins would put it.[4] Surviving, lasting, excelling—these all require vision, planning, and operational excellence, to name just a few. Add consistency to the list, too. For without the discipline to stick to a vision, work a plan, and avoid the "heck, why not?" decisions that come from welcoming any and all opportunities, even great ships run aground.

Remember that The *Disciplined* Entrepreneur knows that it's less important how his or her role is shaped than that the company excels and succeeds, so I want to plant something in your mind for consideration.

One of the most critical roles of the CEO in any organization is improving the company's market value. You may not have spent much time thinking about stock prices as you've been building your company, but it's a factor to consider as you move toward your Second Decision. Those stock certificates aren't just pieces of paper; they're very real, especially to your investors. Why did they invest in you? What sort of return are they expecting on your investment? And, most importantly, who are they relying on for that return? While some responsibilities of leadership can be shared or even delegated, this one is *all yours*. Is it a responsibility you're comfortable shouldering? Can you do more than be comfortable, can you truly embrace it? It's something to think about as you consider becoming a *Qualified* Entrepreneur.

So let's begin with the end in mind! Where might you end up in your self-awareness journey? There are five roles to choose from, and this book will help you discover which choice is best for you. The first three choices relate to the various ways that you, as an entrepreneur, can make yours a more disciplined organization—thus, they all three are *Qualified* Entrepreneur choices. The last two are different; those two are choices that come from recognizing that perhaps you aren't at a place where you can totally commit to becoming a *Qualified* Entrepreneur—or that maybe you're content to keep things as they are now.

COMPONENTS OF THE SECOND DECISION

QUALIFIED ENTREPRENEUR ROLES

1. **The Leader.** This could be the founder, the owner/operator—the captain of the ship, if you will. Regardless of title, this is the *Qualified* Entrepreneur who, at any stage of the company's growth, wants to self-qualify as CEO. He or she has the capabilities and is willing to commit to the work and learning necessary to lead the

company, as well to put the right people in the right seats to support a vision. In this choice, the *Qualified* Entrepreneur, and/or the executive team, is charged with instilling discipline throughout the organization as well as making their own consistent and disciplined leadership decisions.

2. **The Role Player.** This *Qualified* Entrepreneur prefers not to be CEO at all, or wishes to leave that role after a certain point in the growth cycle. The Role Player is willing to hire the right people to operate the company so that he or she can pursue passions inside the company. Alternate roles for the entrepreneur in this choice could include chairman, board member, inventor, chief sales officer, and COO, to name a few.

3. **The Creator.** This *Qualified* Entrepreneur loves the company that he or she has built, but doesn't want to be the CEO. The Creator prefers to hire the right people to operate the business so that he or she can pursue passions outside the company. Entrepreneurs who itch to start multiple companies are the perfect fit here. In addition, this could be the path for a CEO who is ready to retire or turn the business over to a new CEO and move on to some non-entrepreneurial pursuit. In all cases, the Creator understands that it is critically important to leave behind a disciplined company, and that the highest expression of this type is to "pay it forward" as a *Qualified* Entrepreneur who

brings the same structure and commitment to his or her new venture.

ENTREPRENEUR ROLES

4. **The Dabbler.** In this choice, like the one that follows, the entrepreneur remains an entrepreneur. If you choose the role of the Dabbler, you're willing to employ some of the leadership strategies that would move you towards becoming a *Qualified Entrepreneur*, but not all of them. Basically, you like your business life the way it is; you just see the benefit of stepping up your game in a few specific ways. My recommendation is to read this book for assistance in areas where your company may be struggling, skimming for takeaways as you go. My hope is that your movement toward achieving some of the characteristics of being a *Qualified Entrepreneur* takes hold and inspires you to commit fully.

5. **Status Quo.** This choice has the entrepreneur remaining both entrepreneur and CEO, without committing to any changes in leadership or decision-making. My advice? Read another business book that seems more relevant to you. Give this one to somebody you think may enjoy it!

Don't get me wrong. Options 4 and 5 are legitimate choices. Success can be found by these routes, especially in businesses that don't require a lot of managerial complexity. I'd just offer the same warning that consultant and business adviser Ram Charan does in his lectures: maintaining the status quo can actually be a step backwards. In other words, selecting Option 4 or 5 carries the risk that your competitors will include leaders who have chosen Option 1, 2, or 3. Their decision to enhance their skills and create more discipline within their organization could leave your company at a disadvantage.

Having had a look at the components of the Second Decision that will face you at the end of the book, I know it's tempting to start making lists and doing cost-benefit analyses. It's our nature as entrepreneurs to want to get where we're going just as soon as it's clear where the road is headed. But I encourage you to wait and let the following chapters guide you through the sort of assessment you might see conducted by a coach, consultant, or board of directors. Do yourself a favor, though, and start yourself a *Qualified* Entrepreneur (QE) Notebook or create a QE section in any management notebook you're already maintaining. This notebook will accompany you through the chapters ahead, where I will be suggesting items for you to include in it. Not only does your QE Notebook facilitate note taking and planning as you read, it functions as a binder for the critical reports and documents that I believe a *Qualified* Entrepreneur should be reviewing on a regular basis.

That's it. That's all you need to pack for this particular journey. Now let's "begin with the end in mind" and ready ourselves for positive change.

CHAPTER 2 QUAL CARD

Initial each requirement as met:

PREREQUISITES

INITIALS

The entrepreneur acknowledges that the need to consider becoming a *Qualified* Entrepreneur is entirely self-created, owing to the fact that his/her successful business now requires greater leadership and discipline.

_____

The entrepreneur fully understands and acknowledges the four issues that may pose a challenge to his/her efforts to become a *Qualified* Entrepreneur. Check those that apply:

___ Insistence on autonomy

___ Unwillingness to build structure, cultivate expertise, or delegate

___ Boredom

___ Failure to engage in self-examination

_____

The entrepreneur fully understands the three *Qualified* Entrepreneur roles that are the possible outcomes of a Second Decision, and the two additional entrepreneur roles that represent no commitment or a limited commitment to becoming a *Qualified* Entrepreneur.

_____

To recognize his/her primary role in creating shareholder value, the entrepreneur has found and made copies of the company's original stock certificate(s), adding these to the QE Notebook. In addition, the entrepreneur can discuss the current and future value (three years in the future) of the organization and fully explain the trends and reasons behind the growth in stock price.

_____

SIGNATURE: _____

DATE: _____

START BY STOPPING...AND SLOW DOWN TO SPEED UP!

"Vulnerability is the birthplace of innovation, creativity and change"

—BRENÉ BROWN (TED TALK)

I want to congratulate you on making the preliminary decision to become a *Qualified* Entrepreneur! (Yes, I'm assuming this is what you chose!) With your initial Second Decision complete, you're ready to begin the self-awareness journey that this book offers you to help you zero in on which of the three *Qualified* Entrepreneur roles you will eventually choose when your Qual Card is complete.

Your journey begins here as it did for me—with the time and introspection it takes to create a personal timeline. The Entrepreneurs' Organization (EO), Vistage, Young Presidents' Organization (YPO), and other professional organizations I've been part of like to call it a *lifeline*. It's not a buoy tossed from a ship or the phone-a-friend option on *Who Wants to Be a Millionaire?* It's a timeline that depicts the events and achievements of your life.

Our lives can be mapped by graphing our experiences and our activities. Anyone willing to sit down and make a timeline of his or her life can't help but gain a new perspective on why certain periods were successful, and why others were so difficult. Inevitably, the exercise also provides insight into what lies ahead. I know this because I've done it. And, in that sense, the term *lifeline* is pretty apt—the exercise may well save you from making mistakes in your future, especially the old mistakes you've made too many times before!

The first time I encountered the lifeline activity was when I joined the Entrepreneurs' Organization, which was originally known as Young Entrepreneurs' Organization. Creating a lifeline is the method by which EO groups form and bond—you share the good, the bad, and the ugly of your life as you've lived it to that point. Doing this makes everyone a bit vulnerable, opening doors to honest "experience-sharing," as EO calls it. Without that honesty and willingness to share, the group just doesn't gel to achieve its goal—which is providing entrepreneurs a safe place to seek and receive advice. I have seen

> Without that honesty and willingness to share, the group just doesn't gel to achieve its goal—which is providing entrepreneurs a safe place to seek and receive advice. I have seen this exercise work well with CEOs and their executive teams as well.

this exercise work well with CEOs and their executive teams as well.

It really is of benefit to us as entrepreneurs, all of us, to *slow down*— to take more opportunities to look across the whole landscape of what's happened and what's likely to happen, before jumping into action. One of the most productive lessons I have learned in the past two decades is that when I take time to set my game plan, I go two or three times faster and smarter than I do otherwise—and in the actual direction I want to go! I am convinced that you will get far more out of reading this book if you'll . . . *start by stopping*. And slow down to speed up!

YOUR ENTREPRENEURIAL LIFELINE

There are many different kinds of lifelines we could create to reflect who we are and where we've been. We could draw a lifeline that reflects our starting and growing a family, even our patterns of activity in the category of health and fitness over the years. Each of these can be revealing in its own way. But first, let's put our focus on one of the most significant measures of who or what we are—our entrepreneurial careers. Here's my history:

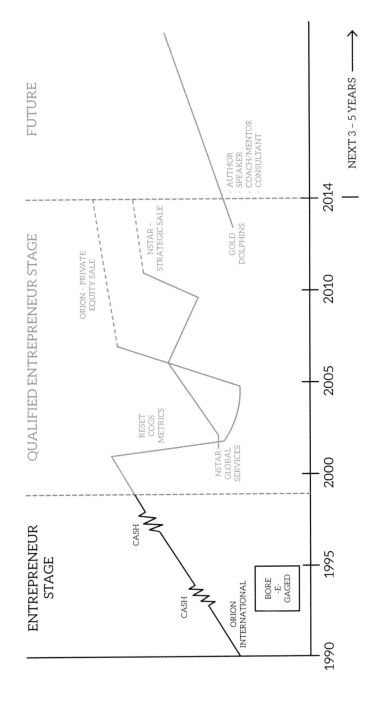

You can see that I started almost 25 years ago, and that I have been involved in five startups to date. Three of the companies are operating as standalones today. A fourth was merged into my first company, Orion International, back in 1996. A fifth was shut down soon after it began in the early 1990s. A quick calculation tells me that's a 20 percent failure rate!

My lifeline shows nothing but growth and investment for my first 10 years as an entrepreneur. See that box marked "Bored Zone?" That's where I got a little stir-crazy and decided to start a second company, the one that didn't last long. That's what I call "bor-e-gaged"—wavering from bored to engaged—which we will talk more about later.

There are two obvious dips in the graph, each representing a significant business downturn. Both recessions were deep enough to threaten the existence of the company I was running at the time. Stemming from the downturns were cash crises, difficulties meeting payroll, and after the first recession hit, about three years of downsizing and restructuring. It was awful. But we survived, and I learned plenty about how to lead and manage a business.

Let's look now at my leadership pattern. I was part of a startup in 2002, and within two years I had stepped away from day-to-day activities in my first business to launch a new one—while retaining my ownership stake in the first. (In terms of *Qualified Entrepreneur* types, that's me choosing Option 2—to be the Role Player—in Orion, which allowed me to become the Creator in NSTAR.) The second of the business downturns I experienced definitely impacted NSTAR, but I benefited from the learning that occurred during the first recession, and I am convinced that the second dip in the graph would have plunged much deeper had I not learned so many lessons in the first, more catastrophic downturn.

Aside from the effects of macroeconomic trends, two of my existing businesses—Orion and NSTAR—followed classic business growth curves, experiencing the ups and downs that most of us know well. Leading these companies was like taking Business 101 for me and my partners, and throughout this book I will be outlining the lessons I've learned and detailing how these lessons will (1) help you avoid becoming a failure statistic, and (2) improve your company's long-term consistency and productivity.

In the end, both Orion and NSTAR succeeded well beyond my expectations. Each achieved the kind of growth that attracts buyers, and both companies were indeed sold—Orion in its 16th year to a *financial buyer*, and NSTAR in its 8th to a *strategic buyer*. Both companies have continued their steady growth patterns since the sale and remain market leaders in their respective industries.

Before we move on to the Qual Card and the next chapter, let me list a few more experiences you may find relevant in understanding my point of view in this book:

- I have been both a majority owner and a minority equal partner. (The terms *I* and *we* are interchangeable in this book. I had partners in both Orion and NSTAR, and without our collective work together we would not have succeeded. It was indeed a team leadership effort!)

- I was a junior officer in the US Navy submarine force for almost seven years, gaining invaluable leadership experience while serving my country.

- For nearly four years after selling NSTAR, I gained invaluable "hands-on education" expanding our business globally in Europe and Asia. Maybe the bigger lesson was figuring out how to function effectively in a multibillion-dollar global firm *as an employee*, not as the owner. In addition, I spent my last year as an "Intrapreneur", given the unique opportunity to develop a potential new business for the global CEO.

- I have chaired, served on, and served under boards of directors for a variety of organizations in the private sector, including some in the nonprofit and philanthropic sector.

- My most recent business, Gold Dolphins, LLC, offers executive coaching and consulting services to entrepreneurs and CEOs. (Of course, I had to choose a company name that reflected being a *Qualified* Entrepreneur. At some point, my goal will be to design the pin that will be given to entrepreneurs who take the challenge to become qualified—I will look for input from you as to what that should be!)

- With this book I am branching out into speaking, and adding "author" to my bio for the first time—all with the aim of sharing with as many entrepreneurs and CEOs as possible what I have learned in becoming a *Qualified* Entrepreneur . . . and creating what I hope will become multitudes of QEs around the world in the future!

But enough about me. Now it's your turn to draw up your own Entrepreneurial Lifelines in the space below. To better visualize trends, draw a rough timeline for your industry and the overall economy, too, as I have. Mark in significant events and particular business struggles.

BUSINESS TIMELINE/LIFELINE

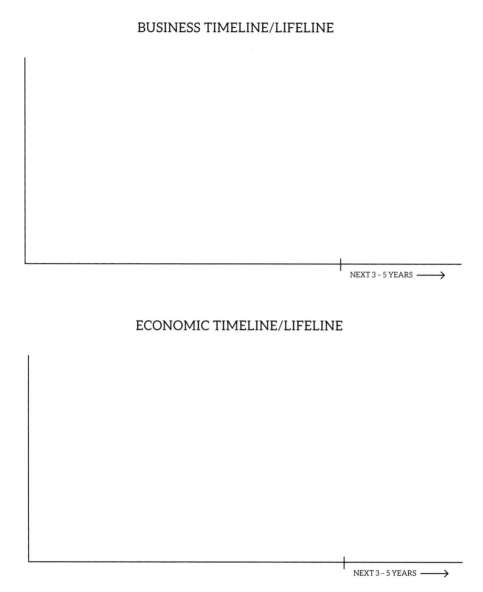

NEXT 3 - 5 YEARS ⟶

ECONOMIC TIMELINE/LIFELINE

NEXT 3 - 5 YEARS ⟶

When the timelines are complete, take a little time to pretend you're standing in front of some peers explaining the graphs. It will clarify your own understanding of where you've been—which, of course, is crucial information for planning a future.

Lastly, I want you to extend your timelines out three to five years, making your best educated guess as to what lies ahead for you. The self-awareness journey I'm taking you on uses your past and present to help you think deeply about what your future should look like. This is the platform from which you'll make the Second Decision at the end of the book: Which role of the *Qualified* Entrepreneur is going to be best for both you and your company? Will you continue to lead? Will you support from a different role or title? Or will you move on to create anew?

CHAPTER 3 QUAL CARD

Initial each requirement as met:

PREREQUISITES INITIALS

The entrepreneur has drawn his/her
Entrepreneurial Lifeline, beginning with
the start date of the first entrepreneurial
venture and including all businesses that
have followed. The lifeline should be a
graphic representation of the highs and
lows in his/her career, and include an
extension out three to five years into the
future. _____

The entrepreneur has created an economic
graph to indicate macroeconomic and
industry-specific trends during the span of
the lifeline. _____

The entrepreneur has imagined himself/
herself explaining the lifeline and the
career it represents to a small group of
entrepreneurial peers. _____

SIGNATURE: _____

DATE: _____

WHAT KIND OF LEADER ARE YOU?

"What is necessary to change a person is to change his awareness of himself."

—ABRAHAM MASLOW

Most of us think we know ourselves pretty well. Especially as we age and become more experienced in the game of life, we gain a pretty good understanding of what we like and don't, how we view the world socially and politically, whether we're big-city or small-town at heart, and so on. And right there at the top of our list is the fact that we are entrepreneurs or CEOs or growth-minded business people, with all the attributes those words convey. Man, when I walk into an Entrepreneurs' Organization or Vistage meeting, I'm totally at ease—these are my people!

So what a surprise it was one summer not long ago, when I was faced with the fact that the entrepreneurs I feel most comfortable with . . . are actually quite different from me, and from one another. It had me asking a very basic question:

"IS THERE SUCH A THING AS AN ENTREPRENEURIAL PERSONALITY?"

After that particular day, my answer has to be no. There are almost endless variations of the general type, but no one single entrepreneurial personality.

I realized this when a business associate and friend, John Grinnell, CEO of Grinnell Leadership in Chapel Hill, conducted a retreat for my peer group. It was a session based on the Myers-Briggs personality profile and the PRF—the Personality Research Form from Sigma Assessment Systems, Inc. The PRF was introduced in 1967 and still represents a major breakthrough in psychological testing today.

I'd bet most of us are familiar with the Myers-Briggs[1] and DISC,[2] another popular assessment tool, and probably have taken one of these tests (or something similar) at least once. But I was less familiar with the PRF and had never seen the results delivered the way John delivered them.[3] He set up chairs in a semicircle, and for each of the categories, we lined up from left to right, highest to lowest score. New category? New chairs for everybody. Wow. Never would I have guessed that people who have so much in common could score so differently.

Look at some of the personality traits that the PRF evaluates (which I've tried to define):

- Achievement (big goals do or don't energize me)

- Aggression (attitude toward competition)

- Affiliation (interest in being with other people, as in teams)

- Change (ability to deal with it)

- Dominance (whether we relish being in charge)

- Endurance (stamina and follow-through in meeting goals)

- Nurturance (attitude toward guiding and caring for people)

- Exhibition (level of comfort with being seen in public)

- Autonomy (a measure of comfort with and without supportive structure)

I had plenty of reality checks that day. I thought, wrongly, that each of us would be as competitive as the next, and that all of us would love being in charge. We're entrepreneurs, aren't we? Well, just because I love to be the captain of my ship and I thrive on competition doesn't mean others feel the same. The exercise clearly showed us that we are very different individuals who lead our organizations in varied ways. Some are clearly top-dog, instilling discipline and operational excellence by using their own personality as an example. Some function much better as the head of a team. Some function best with structure built into the organization, while others avoid it like the plague. To my surprise, there were many whose scores indicated

> I thought, wrongly, that each of us would be as competitive as the next, and that all of us would love being in charge.

they were far more comfortable being taken care of *by* people than taking care of people.

As the session unfolded, I couldn't help but wonder whose personality was best suited to their task—the hard-driving Type-A CEO, or somebody who put personal values and the needs of his or her employees ahead of everything, maybe even including growth? There seemed to be no easy way to say what was "good" or "bad." There were just differences. And, for the first time, I could clearly see that a *Qualified* Entrepreneur—a concept that was growing in my mind—could and *should* consider various career paths after the entrepreneurial startup phase. The results I saw that day showed that some of us should **lead**, some of us should **support**, and some of us should continue to **create**. I wouldn't propose that a single test's results be used to slot you, me, or anybody else—but the data is undoubtedly good to have. PRF results offer a good signpost, if you will, for the self-awareness journey you're undertaking through this book.

Through the PRF (and Myers-Briggs, DISC, and so on) I've learned a lot about my personality. I've learned that it is important for me to set ambitious goals, that I need space in which to operate, that I'm okay with structure (as opposed to full autonomy), and that I'm at my best when I'm with people. I also learned some fun stuff—like why I don't care to skydive, especially at this time of my life. I just don't get that big a thrill from risk for risk's sake, I guess. But, man, some of my friends are fearless! (Yes, Paul, I am talking about you!)

Given that one of everybody's favorite subjects is themselves, maybe it isn't a surprise how much I enjoyed becoming better acquainted with my personality. But the PRF did more than satisfy my curiosity or give me talking points with friends. It was a major development in my decision to become a *Qualified* Entrepreneur, as I'm confident it will be in yours. None other than self-help author Stephen R. Covey advocates for self-awareness.[4] Here's how he defines it: "*. . . the ability to reflect on one's own life, grow in self-knowledge, and to use that knowledge to improve oneself and either overcome or compensate for weaknesses.*"

So, lay the foundation for greater self-awareness to come: take the PRF (or Myers-Briggs or DISC tests) if you haven't, or do it again if you have. The link on my website will make it very easy for you to complete the PRF and get your results—and be sure to get the PRF Personality Profile as part of your feedback.

None other than self-help author Stephen R. Covey advocates for self-awareness. Here's how he defines it: "*. . . the ability to reflect on one's own life, grow in self-knowledge, and to use that knowledge to improve oneself and either overcome or compensate for weaknesses.*"

ARE CEO'S AND ENTREPRENEURS ALIKE?

I've done my own little experiment on that question over the last few years. I've been asking my leadership peers to choose a few words to describe an entrepreneur. Here are the perennial vote-getters:

- Crazy/Fearless

- Creative/Innovative

- Energetic/Driven

- Risk taking

- Maverick/Independent

- Visionary

- Intelligent

Hmm. Not surprising, but interesting. Now, notice what happens when I substitute "CEO" for "entrepreneur":

- Leader/Boss

- Organized

- Responsible/Steady

- Communication/People skills

- Disciplined

- Visionary

- Intelligent

What catches my eye is that "Visionary" and "Intelligent" make both lists, but the other descriptors are strikingly different. I think it's also interesting that none of the people I polled has "Entrepreneur" as the title on their business card. Instead, it's President,

CEO, or Founder. Doesn't this suggest that we view entrepreneurship as a core that we add layers to as our companies grow and our leadership challenges become more complex? That it's something we maintain, yet grow beyond?

I can't help but notice that CEOs get labeled "disciplined," but entrepreneurs don't. What this tells me is that most of us acknowledge that CEOs work in bigger organizations than do entrepreneurs, and that what this means is that the leader can't know or "touch" every employee anymore. To lead a larger and more fully managed company, a leader must provide vision and exhibit a rigorous devotion to planning, goals, and accountabilities—in other words, *discipline*. A CEO, you might say (and I certainly would), needs to be a *Qualified* Entrepreneur.

> To lead a larger and more fully managed company, a leader must provide vision and exhibit a rigorous devotion to planning, goals, and accountabilities—in other words, *discipline*. A CEO, you might say (and I certainly would), needs to be a *Qualified* Entrepreneur.

Until now, we entrepreneurs have had to let chance and circumstance shape us into the leaders our companies require. We have had to hope for good instincts or skilled mentoring, if we were to successfully guide our companies through growth to maturity. Unlike the US Navy and some similarly rigorous, training-oriented careers, there has been no process by which we entrepreneurs can become qualified to lead. That's why I'm taking a stab at it here in this book. I want to share with you the ports of call on my own voyage to becoming a *Qualified* Entrepreneur. This includes the things I learned the hard way, the strategies I stumbled upon and found helpful in my OJT (on-the-job training) days, and the ways of managing that I gleaned from a host of workshops, my peer groups, seminars, and bedtime reading—and then put to the test in my own companies.

Now, if you and I are honest with ourselves, we know that we entrepreneurs can be enthusiastic listeners and learners who… do a fairly lousy job of implementation. Yes, the people who so pride themselves in their "bias for action" are sometimes slow or downright unwilling to institute change. How will this book change the outcome? Well, first, you're only working with yourself here. It's a *self-awareness journey* through which you evaluate your skills and interests in each key aspect of managing a growth company. You've already made an educated guess at where you'll be when the Second Decision arrives at the end of this book, but you won't be committing to any type of change until you've reached that point—and even then, only *you* will know what you considered, chose, or ruled out. There will be nothing telltale on your calendar, and no company cohorts taking in the same information and pressing you to do something with it.

INTRODUCING ... LEADERSHIP PERSONALITY TYPES

To this point in the chapter, we've determined that all entrepreneurs aren't alike, and that a CEO is typically seen as bringing more structure to running a company than an entrepreneur. Now I want to slice things a little differently. I want to talk about the personality types that live within the general categories of entrepreneur or CEO. My goal? Self-awareness, of course.

I think there are ways of understanding ourselves when we process new information or face a challenge—and that we can internalize and use this self-knowledge to help us recognize when our personality and our approach to management is affecting our choices or preventing us from acting. Throughout this book, I'll be referencing four different entrepreneurial personality types. Here they are, in brief:

- **Urgent/Reactive:** "Fix it and forget it" —someone who is always two steps behind.

- **Ever Optimistic:** "Things are great!" —someone who is either one step ahead or one step behind.

- **Reflexively Pessimistic:** "Batten down the hatches!" —someone who is either one step ahead or one step behind.

- **Steady/Proactive:** "I'm as ready as I can be for the challenges I'll be facing" —someone who is always two steps ahead.

The names may or may not work for you, but I think we all recognize the types.

The **Urgent/Reactive** leader creates and thrives on an almost crazed atmosphere, where he or she can ride to the rescue, put out the fire, be everybody's savior, then move on to the next problem—in other words, fix it and forget it. By virtue of being so busy, Urgent/Reactive is the classic sort of "I Don't Know What I Don't Know" (IDKWIDK) leader. There isn't time for introspection. There is no vision to be served, no plan to be implemented. All of that falls secondary to the need to grow and keep up with growth. The hours are long in companies with a leader such as this. Lunch is always eaten at the desk, because it bolsters that sense of extreme busyness. And there's the boss, forever bouncing from issue to issue and emergency to emergency like some sort of overworked first responder—who just happens to be, habitually, about two steps behind where he or she ought to be to properly lead the organization. Yet, it can be a satisfying management style for all concerned. At the end of the day, there is a feeling of accomplishment for the CEO and employees alike, simply because it's been so darned busy.

I saw a version of this when I was a US Navy lieutenant. Watching my boss, an Urgent/Reactive type who thrived on micromanaging and being Mr. Fix-it, I learned exactly what not to do. He measured productivity by hours worked, period. He actually positioned his desk so he could monitor everyone's activities all day… so he would always be ready to pounce if something went wrong. He knew when they came in, and he took note of when they left. Excellence, to him, was measured by how overworked he could keep his people. I vowed never to lead that way, and I've kept my promise. Not enough hours in the day, you say? Get more efficient at managing your time, I'd tell you. Why eat your lunch at your desk every day—and force your people to do the same—when you could be working out at the gym or enjoying a sunshine break?

As entrepreneurs—or perhaps newly elevated leaders in an existing organization—we all start with Urgent/Reactive tendencies. Leadership of this sort isn't taught to most of us; we just jump in and get going. We do what we think will look and feel most effective. We don't consider new ways of leading and managing until somebody or something slows us down and makes us stop to think.

I remember my wife turning to me once, eight years into my business career, to ask a simple, pointed question: "Do you know what you're doing?" At the time I was expanding the offices of my first company from three to nine. I felt on top of the world, so I didn't hesitate a moment before replying, "Yes!" But the truth was, I Didn't Know What I Didn't Know (IDKWIDK). Soon

The truth was, I Didn't Know What I Didn't Know (IDKWIDK).

after, I attended my first serious management seminar (the EO Birthing of Giants program that I will describe in a future chapter), and it became almost painfully clear how much I still had to learn. That is why I have never forgotten that moment with my wife. And when my company experienced the challenges of a major economic downturn, I once again saw a significant gap between what I knew and what I needed to know. It was during these challenges that I made and reinforced my commitment to the continual work of increasing one's personal capacity as a leader—if not day by day, then certainly year by year. These were my moments of reckoning. Have you had yours yet?

Now that we've been formally introduced to Urgent/Reactive, someone we all have at least a nodding familiarity with, let's meet the other entrepreneurial personality types we'll be referring to in the chapters ahead.

From a leadership perspective, **Ever Optimistic** and **Reflexively Pessimistic** are the sunny and cloudy sides of the same personality. I'm probably a little more familiar with the sunny side, but I've known the cloudy one as well. Ever Optimistic's favorite phrases are "I'm doing great!" and "Things are terrific!" Reflexively Pessimistic, meanwhile, lives in a defensive crouch and can always give you chapter and verse on why things have been, are, and likely always will be so challenging.

> The researchers found that entrepreneurs start businesses because they're convinced that they have the sense, smarts, or sheer luck it takes to avoid catastrophe.

These two managerial stances come from very different CEO psychologies.

Ever Optimistic starts from the belief that there is nothing he or she can't do. There's a lot of it going around, apparently, because a 1997 study in the *Journal of Business Venturing* found that the key identifier when it comes to entrepreneurs isn't risk seeking, it's self-confidence. The researchers found that entrepreneurs start businesses because they're convinced that they have the sense, smarts, or sheer luck it takes to avoid catastrophe. Then, if the entrepreneur has the good fortune to experience a period of unfettered growth or a persistent economic up-cycle, look out! The boss will soon be humming "We Are the Champions." I've been there. In the first eight years of my first business, Orion International's revenues grew 50 percent year over year, convincing me I could do no wrong. When someone asked me about my business, I responded by describing growing numbers of employees and locations, and all the new business ideas I was vetting. The only thing that kept me up at night was trying to figure out how to keep pace with the growth. My persistently upbeat view of the situation—and my steadfast refusal to think the outlook would ever change—made the environment a happy and fulfilling one for me and my employees. My key managerial tool was inspiration. The sheer enthusiasm I demonstrated on a daily basis was contagious and motivating. But all of that changed for me, as it does for most managers of the Ever Optimistic type, when my business slowed almost to a standstill due to macroeconomic trends. Typically, it's only then that it becomes clear whether the Ever Optimistic boss is a step ahead of where he or she should be in leading the business, or an equal amount behind.

As aggressively as the Ever Optimistic leader plays offense, the **Reflexively Pessimistic** CEO plays defense—not to win, but to survive. Indeed, the offense never really gets any playing time in a Reflexively Pessimistic leader's operation. He or she has been made tough by hard times, and so is persistently worried about the economy's effect on the business. Look around and you'll see plenty of organizations that are still living the last economic crisis; they are hunkered down and almost paralyzed by fear of moving forward. If the industry is an easily battered one, such as finance or construction, this management approach is a legitimate strategy.

But if maintained for too long, the CEO's pessimistic point of view becomes a self-fulfilling prophesy.

Whereas Ever Optimistic CEOs lead with their enthusiasm, Reflexively Pessimistic CEOs guide and are guided by information. This type of CEO puts painstaking effort into tracking economic indicators and industry-specific measures of trouble. Having a more operational point of view than most CEOs, the tendency of those who are Reflexively Pessimistic is to first think through why things can't or won't work. He or she will focus obsessively on margin to the exclusion of opportunity, for example. The risk of being a (operationally excellent but offensively challenged) Reflexively Pessimistic CEO is the possibility of falling many steps behind the innovators who are creating the future in their industries and beyond.

> The risk of being a (operationally excellent but offensively challenged) Reflexively Pessimistic CEO is the possibility of falling many steps behind the innovators who are creating the future in their industries and beyond.

As in most things, a little moderation would go a long way for both of these personality types. As one CEO put it after having gained some perspective, "I was never as good as I thought I was when business was booming. But I was never as bad as I thought I was when business sucked."

This brings us to the **Steady/Proactive** leader, the type we should all be aiming to become. Such leaders are highly respected and much sought after, because they value productivity above all things and understand how to achieve it. They can course-correct whatever the weather. They understand both offense and defense, and shift comfortably between them as cycles dictate. This type of CEO very much knows what he or she does and doesn't know, using that knowledge to hire the right talent and promote the most skilled. Steady/Proactive is also a manager who has moved beyond a revenue-only focus and now devotes time and effort to understanding what boosts stock value, using this knowledge to push the valuation ever higher.

Steady/Proactive also understands an important paradox: sometimes an organization needs to slow down to vision and plan before it can speed up for successful growth. Therefore, the single most identifying characteristic of this highly skilled CEO is that he or she has taken the time to lay out a three-year vision, one that drives a robust planning regimen. This consists of a one-year plan, a set of quarterly goals, and various initiatives to bring it all to fruition. We'll take up these leadership tasks in the next chapter. It's coming up right after your Qual Card signature for this chapter.

CHAPTER 4 QUAL CARD

Initial each requirement as met:

PREREQUISITES INITIALS

The entrepreneur has gone online to take
the PRF (Personality Research Form),
obtained a complete printout, and placed
a copy in the QE Notebook. The PRF is
available on my website. In addition, here
is the link for taking the Myers-Briggs. See:
https://www.mbticomplete.com/en/index.
aspx.

_____

The entrepreneur has become familiar
with the four types of CEO leadership
introduced in this chapter: Urgent/
Reactive, Ever Optimistic, Reflexively Pessimistic, and Steady/Proactive. The entrepreneur has assessed which type or types
pertain to him/her in various contexts of
leadership, recognizing that while some
types will predominate, few if any CEOs
will fit just one category.

_____

SIGNATURE: _____

DATE: _____

HOW TO DEVELOP AND BRIEF YOUR THREE-YEAR VISION

"The toughest thing about being a success is that you've got to keep on being a success"

—IRVING BERLIN

Let's imagine that this afternoon you are scheduled to convene your annual company meeting. The main agenda item is your hour-long presentation to employees, during which you'll brief them on your vision for the business. It's probably the most formally organized and important event of your corporate year. To be more specific, this afternoon you will be unveiling your three-year plan for all to see.

In Jim Collins blockbuster book *Built to Last* he includes Core Ideology (Core Purpose and Core Values) and an Envisioned Future (10 to 30 year BHAG and Vivid Description) as part of his Vision framework.[1] For the Second Decision, my focus will rest solely on the three-year vision (plan) each and every one of us entrepreneurs must have to move forward as a *Qualified* Entrepreneur.

Even if you've never been part of a dog-and-pony show on Wall Street or made a pitch to a would-be investor, you know the drill for a command performance like this: dress for success, be friendly but authoritative, keep your remarks clear and succinct, anticipate questions and concerns, and, as much as you can, let the product sell itself. That's how you get financing or sell securities firms on your initial public offering (IPO). To a large extent, it's also how you sell your employees on your corporate vision. Just as investors know what they're looking for in your business plan—your employees, too, know whether you're worth their expenditure of time and energy.

This is by no means an idle concern. Coming out of the most recent recession, it has been estimated that as many as 80 percent of employed people in the United States are less than fully satisfied with their current employment, and, even if they're not actively looking, they are open to considering new jobs. (Right Management conducted that survey of 411 workers in the United States and Canada in 2013.[2]) A CareerBuilder survey published in 2014 revealed that 21 percent of full-time US employees are resolved to find a new job *during that year*—the largest number yet for the post-recession era.[3] The expected rise in turnover seems related to job dissatisfaction that has grown as the economy has picked up and made it more feasible for people to consider changing employment.[4, 5]

So, look around the office. Can you stand to lose up to a fifth of your workforce? Even one or two lost employees can cause the business to incur costs related to hiring and training—costs you'd rather avoid. After today's meeting, will your employees feel your company is worth another year of their investment? Or will your inability to inform and inspire send them rushing to the exits to, in effect, sell?

An event of this importance requires preparation. Weeks or months before you take the podium, you should have readied yourself for today's meeting by doing a careful review of that corporate vision of yours. Are you pleased with it? Is it solid enough to withstand tough questioning? Does it inspire?

Do you even have a vision? I don't mean a lazy vision; I mean a real one.

> After today's meeting, will your employees feel your company is worth another year of their investment? Or will your inability to inform and inspire send them rushing to the exits to, in effect, sell?

The easiest "vision" for an entrepreneur or CEO to achieve is one that simply projects current revenue and profit for three years using the current growth rate. The more difficult decision, by far, is to truly sit down and figure out not just what your vision should entail, but how to achieve it…and that's the process of the *Qualified* Entrepreneur.

WHY YOUR VISION IS EVERYTHING

There is nothing more important in a CEO's portfolio than the job of creating, carrying, and communicating the company's vision. You can break this mission into many parts, of course.

But the key part is the vision's ability to move ourselves and our companies beyond the tactical thinking of entrepreneurship, where everything is new and there's more of it to deal with every five minutes. Beyond that crazed and all-too-familiar world is the strategic world of the *Qualified* Entrepreneur, where the boss has combined the multifaceted skills and the long-term perspective necessary to be a successful CEO. You have to be able to see the future, understand how to achieve it, *and* . . . be able to explain it to your employees, your customers, and your investors. Those who lead with a vision that is backed up by plans to achieve it are, indeed, the "two steps ahead" leaders.

I hope that a question is forming in your mind, and it's one that will persist in the self-awareness journey you're taking through this book: *What value are you, as leader, bringing to your organization?*

What this means is: Are you really prepared to lead and listen? To guard and promote the vision? To inspire the passion necessary to achieve it? Or, are you rather half-heartedly fulfilling the role of CEO because you're the one who started the company, bought it, or was born into it?

These questions are not meant to be confrontational. I'm just trying to help you qualify yourself for the position you hold, much as my superiors in the US Navy made me prove my qualifications to drive a submarine, item by item, on my own US Navy Qual Card. Can you imagine the damage that I'd have caused the submarine without having proven myself before taking the helm?

Here's how I think of it: as entrepreneurs and CEOs, it's our job to be good judges of value—product value, market value, employee value, you name it. I'm asking each of us—and I am definitely including myself in this—to pause now and then to consider our own value, using the various metrics of management. *Where in our skill set is the stock high? Where's it in a slump? How should you invest in yourself to ensure that the market invests in your company, and your employees invest in you?*

Intel CEO Andy Grove famously posed this hypothetical question to Intel cofounder Gordon Moore in 1985 when the company's memory chip business was under siege: "If we got kicked out and the board brought in a new CEO, what would he [or she] do?"[6] So what would they do in your current organization, and does your current vision mirror those decisions?

"If we got kicked out and the board brought in a new CEO, what would he [or she] do?" So what would they do in your current organization, and does your current vision mirror those decisions?

Creating a vision is the first and biggest step in enhancing your value to your company. A vision channels your energies and reduces your likelihood of making strategic mistakes. For the company as a whole, vision provides focus and stimulates creative energy. With great execution, the result is enhanced revenue, productivity, and profitability. Besides, without a game plan to offer, a way-to-win that you can present to employees, what on earth will you say at the annual company meeting? How will you spur your people to action in each new fiscal year to come? How will you gain *their* commitment, if not by demonstrating to them *yours*?

HOW TO CREATE YOUR VISION

Visioning begins with the obvious question—and it's one that I regularly ask myself, my coaching clients, and my peers:

"What does success look like—to you—three years from today?"

To move an organization forward, to bring it to its full potential, this question has to be answered in the right way—with well-defined and easy-to-measure goals. It's all well and good to have a goal of "dominat(ing) today, tomorrow and in the future," but as entrepreneurs on a path toward our Second Decision, we should strive for more specificity. So, what are you prepared to dominate? How will you achieve domination? What mileposts can you identify on the road to domination, and how will you measure your ultimate success?

In a way, it's like the seawater question the Captain asked before entrusting me to drive his sub. To answer, you need a broad overview of the entire system, be it a submarine's or a company's. A CEO gains that bird's-eye view by investigating every aspect of the business and its competitive environment. So let's delve deeper into the questions you should have already begun asking yourself as you develop and fine-tune your vision for the future:

- What are the trends in my industry and the economy, *and why?*

- What further changes do I expect to occur in the competitive landscape, *and why?*

- How will I establish and build clear, defendable differentiators in my market space, *and why?*

- What will my product and service portfolio look like in the future? How will it be different from today's portfolio? *And why?*

- What are the trends in my customer base—are they adding or consolidating vendors, looking for partners who can do full service for them, or what? *And why?*

- How will my sandbox change (where I choose to operate/dominate)? How many offices/locations do I envision operating, and where? *And why?*

- How will the structure and makeup of my organization change in the years ahead, *and why?*

- Which key metrics will I track to build the company, *and why?*

- Does my future vision include only organic growth, or am I also committing to mergers and acquisitions or seeking outside investment? *And why?*

- What are my trends, positive or negative, in areas such as finance, customer growth, productivity, employee, and customer satisfaction, and so on? *And why?*

- What sort of revenue and profit goals should I be setting for the next few years, *and why?*

We all know that in sales you don't normally close on the first visit. To get the buyer to remember you . . . and *listen* to you . . . they have to hear from you something like 7–10 times. So, please know that I didn't keep saying "*and why?*" to annoy you. I did it so it would truly sink in how important the "whys" of our businesses are.

Having spent some time pondering these questions and their ramifications, you'll be ready to tease out a handful of **key initiatives**. These will, according to your data, lead to the kind of growth, market domination, and profit you wish to achieve over the next three years. Thus, these key initiatives are the pillars of your overall vision for the company. For these initiatives to be the right ones, they need to be quantifiable. They should be the kind that can propel your organization forward not only from the standpoint of revenue and profit, but also in terms of your ability to compete. You will want to be able to see that you are growing your market share and, as an organization, building defendable differentiators. In other words, you will need to be certain that your vision is grounded in reality and capable of coming to life.

TAKE OFF THE ROSE-COLORED GLASSES!

When identifying key initiatives, don't let yourself be led astray by indulging in revisionist corporate history, or projecting overly rosy views of the future. What I always tell myself is, "The future can become what I want it to be, but the past is what it is—so learn from it!" Don't be the CEO that shows the company's future as a J curve (steady growth to date, followed by a huge jump in the next three years)—unless you can truly justify an unprecedented expansion, of course! Don't just look at today's growth rate and project it forward, either. Keep in mind that every key initiative you propose to establish requires a clear-eyed and, ideally, data-backed review.

The true test of a well-prepared vision comes when the CEO has to show company-level metrics that support the overall plan and make sense, and are not on the J curve just mentioned.

The best way to ensure that you're not pulling the wool over anybody's eyes, especially your own, is to give others a chance to review your work. A visioning exercise may start out solitary, in your own head, but it can't be completed without input from key personnel and perhaps some trusted advisers. You need the informed perspective of others to ensure that real, previously collected data is used to confront the truth of the company's current condition, no matter how uncomfortable or even brutal it may be to face it. You also need the insight of others to test your view of the future, because rose-colored glasses are well known to be blurry!

Last but not least, you need the involvement of interested observers to help you answer the "*and why?*" at the end of each of the above questions. Only then will you know everything you need to know to describe your corporate vision to new employees, investors, peers, key customers, . . . and yes, to the entire assembly of your organization at an annual company-wide meeting. Only then will you be able to answer the amended version of the big question

I presented above: **"What does success look like to you three years from today…*and why*?"**

DANGER AHEAD!

Here's how to tell if you'll end up shortsighted on your three-year vision (plan):

- Your three-year vision can be accomplished in two years, one year, or even sooner. It ends up being more a tactical plan than a strategic one.

- The key initiatives are too general and not quantifiable (for example, *improved* customer service, *more* and *better* employees, *increased* sales revenue).

- The accountability for the vision rests at a level lower than CEO. From my experience observing entrepreneurial CEOs, they love to set goals that keep the target off their own backs. That way the boss never leaves his or her comfort zone and always has someone else to blame. Don't be that CEO!

- The vision is written from the perspective of today's roadblocks and challenges. Unless you can sideline today's worries, which won't be the same as tomorrow's, you won't find your way to a clear and motivating vision. Adding to this, a one-year plan is built *forward* from today's knowledge, rather than it being built *backwards* from the goals of the three-year vision.

- The vision went directly from your brain to the printer with no stops in between. How well does it work when somebody else makes plans without seeking *your* input?

The sheer reluctance we feel when asked to really plant a flag with our vision and make plans to bring it to fruition explains why one-year goals are far more common than three-year visions. It's much easier to start with where things are today and simply make an educated guess as to where the company will be in a year than it is to start from where you should be in Year Three and figure out how to get there from today.

NO "YEAR TWO" ALLOWED!

My observation is that most entrepreneurs do one of two things: either they set a three-year revenue target with *no* key initiatives to back it up (and expect their employees to fill in the blanks on how to get there) or they simply build the three-year "vision" by plotting out Years One, Two, and Three with reasonable growth built into the numbers. Neither type requires much strategy.

What each of us ought to be aiming for is a *vision* leading to a *plan* with *key initiatives* that will be explained, understood, and implemented up and down the pyramid. I'm not the oracle here; many management consultants recommend exactly this. What I'm trying to offer is the inside perspective on why this doesn't always happen, from someone who has lived and continues to live the challenging reality of leadership, both in my own companies and in the hundreds of companies I have observed with my peers over the past 15 years.

The truth is, where visioning and planning is concerned, too many of us start at the end with the beginning in mind (if you'll pardon me reversing the saying). No doubt it seems more practical to get the ball rolling by looking at where things are today and developing a strategy that doesn't speculate too far into the future. But it's far, far more productive to begin with the end in mind. You can't get to where you're going without knowing and really understanding where it is you want to go. You can have the best people in the world working for you (and I hope you do), but if you lack vision, if you haven't planned, and if you haven't established a way of executing to achieve your plans, you will be just like every underperforming sports team with talent but no championship ring. And you know what eventually happens to the coaches of such teams, don't you?

> The truth is, where visioning and planning is concerned, too many of us start at the end with the beginning in mind (if you'll pardon me reversing the saying).

This is why I recommend that CEOs be disallowed from projecting Year Two: I don't want you leaving money on the table! I want to steer you away from any Urgent/Reactive tendencies that are keeping you from being the visionary for your organization. I want you to see no choice but to establish a clear picture of what success looks like three years out and to have key initiatives clearly outlined and in place. Then I want you to build a one-year plan that will move you one year closer to your three-year vision (plan).

Do nothing with Year Two at this point. In a company with a well thought-out vision, Year Two largely takes care of itself.

Here's another reason that I outlaw the planning of Year Two: it not only forces you to create a vision, but to trust that that it is the right one. (*You'd better trust it, because your one-year plan will be based on it!*) Now, if the very thought of committing so fully to a vision puts your stomach in knots, that's good—it probably should. It indicates that you've bumped against the barrier that protects you from everything that lies outside your comfort zone. But ignoring the discomfort and moving forward is definitely part of the journey of becoming a *Qualified* Entrepreneur.

> Here's another reason that I outlaw the planning of Year Two: it not only forces you to create a vision, but to trust that that it is the right one. (*You'd better trust it, because your one-year plan will be based on it!*)

FIND YOURSELF ON THE VISION/ PLANNING SPECTRUM

I've graphed out a comparison of where you are as a leader (are you two steps ahead, two steps behind, or somewhere in between?) and what that says about your plans and your vision. I've also included the likely response of the people you lead at each level of management performance. (Note the grading could be completed by anybody in your organization that holds you accountable, such as a board of directors, coach, or consultant.)

CEO Plan	CEO Value (And Why?)	Performance Rating	Where Are You?	Next Grading Period— Board of Directors (BOD)	Employee Response
Three-year/ one-year plan is in place	Vision is in place	A	2 steps ahead	Promote	Excited/ passionate
Specific one-year plan is in place	Partial vision in place	B	1 step ahead	Train and promote	"I'm in, but I want to see more."
General one-year plan is in place	CEO is sitting in his/her comfort zone	C	On the same step	Train	On the bubble
"A quarterly plan is all we can manage."	"I'm too busy!"	D	1 step behind	Counsel— train	"Why am I listening to you?"
Today's plan may or may not be in place	Banking on hope and hope alone.	F	2 steps behind	Progressive discipline	On Monster. com this afternoon

If your company has a three-year vision that you consider thoughtful and solid, you will be among the minority of CEOs who are ready to turn the focus to a one-year goal, then on to quarterly targets. If you're among the many who haven't arrived at a disciplined three-year vision, start where you're stuck—with the longer-term vision. This isn't something you can do halfway or postpone. Yes, I'm sure there are plenty of issues that are more operational than strategic weighing on your mind, and we'll get to them in this book. But trust me on this; the vision needs to come first.

WHERE DO YOU STAND?

Here is a guided exercise aimed at pinning down where your company stands and helping you move it forward:

In pretty good shape: If you have a three-year vision, a set of key initiatives, and a one-year plan in place, that's great. But are they the right ones? Can you convince yourself that the process by which you established these plans was rigorous and led to the right result? Did you involve the appropriate stakeholders? Are these plans in writing? Have they been well communicated to your company? How can you tell whether your employees have bought into the vision and are putting energy into achieving its goals? Most importantly, are the vision and its associated plans making your decision making noticeably easier? If not, you may have missed the mark.

Behind the curve: If you don't have a three-year vision, the key initiatives, and a one-year plan in place, ask yourself why not. Then listen critically to the answer. If it goes something like "It's on my list; I just haven't had time to get to it yet," believe me, you're not alone. But I'd encourage you to consider what you'd say if one of your employees gave you an answer like that. As I've said, focusing exclusively on the cares and concerns of today is a common problem in business leadership. Unfortunately, when you only see the roadblocks, you miss all the potential avenues that lead to success. My advice to anybody stuck in such a negative frame of mind is to find whatever is your personal "think spot"— Starbucks, an airplane at 35,000 feet, or a hiking trail—and allow yourself the opportunity to dream. Forget the plans; they will come. Just get yourself in the zone, as an athlete would. Find flow. Once you find yourself in the zone, allow zero interruptions, and keep dreaming and envisioning. When you fall out of the zone, immediately write down your thoughts in detail to ensure you keep the gold that you just discovered. Focus on getting a clear, quantifiable vision of what your company should look like in three years. Then start working on it with key employees you trust at all levels of your organization. Try to achieve a sort of corporate ratification. Then *live it.*

Articulating a muscular vision for your company takes the kind of work that never really ends—especially the communication part! *Truly committing to it is, in my opinion, an unparalleled act of corporate courage.* You can't delegate the uncomfortable responsibility of this role. You have to be the one in your organization who will establish where the company is going and how it will get there. If you're an entrepreneur just getting started on your effort to become a *Qualified* Entrepreneur, and you tend toward the Ever Optimistic side of the street, your tendency may be to establish overly lofty goals that will fail not because they're too lofty, necessarily, but because there's no factual justification for the aims and no planning to back them up. On the other hand, if you're an operations person by nature or experience and maybe

> You have to be the one in your organization who will establish where the company is going and how it will get there.

more Reflexively Pessimistic, your vision will likely skew too conservative, because you're stuck worrying what may go wrong. What I've seen work most often, both in my own career and in that of others, is the middle approach. You need to dream for your organization, and reach higher than your employees think possible. At the same time, you have to ensure that the dream—the vision—is backed by objectivity, and combined with quantifiable, attainable goals that aren't generic or easy. It's hard, but it's worthwhile.

As leader of your organization, you need to be comfortable holding the fortunes of the enterprise in your very hands. Every question asked of you should lead back to your vision of the company's future. And every answer should be sufficiently passionate to leave no doubt that the company can and will achieve its goals. You may believe your own words when you make up an answer or feign enthusiasm, but your employees won't. So spare them the platitudes. Be the coach they want you to be. Give them a game plan far more strategic than merely telling them to just increase sales 20 percent this year. Add value as their CEO by carrying a solid vision, communicating it, and, above all, committing to it. That's being a *Qualified* Entrepreneur.

Let the dog-and-pony show begin! You and your company are a stock that is for sale on an open labor market. After your presentation at the company-wide meeting today, will your employees buy, hold, or sell their stock in you?

CHAPTER 5 QUAL CARD

Initial each requirement as met:

PREREQUISITES

The entrepreneur has listed the three to
five major changes that a replacement CEO
would make to his/her company within
12 months of taking over, and offered a
full explanation as to why the changes
would be implemented, as well as why the
current CEO is not making those changes.
The entrepreneur has placed a copy of this
analysis in the QE Notebook.   _____

The entrepreneur has set one-year and
three-year plans for the company and put
them in writing in the QE Notebook.   _____

The entrepreneur has evaluated his/her
performance in visioning, using the A to
F scale in the chart from this chapter and
added a copy to the QE Notebook. The
entrepreneur understands the level and
depth of knowledge expected of the CEO
by his/her accountability partner (the
board of directors, coaches, consultants, or
advisers) in regard to the three-year vision
for the organization.   _____

The entrepreneur can fully explain his/
her visioning process for the future and
has a plan in place to achieve a performance rating of A when visioning is
complete.   _____

The entrepreneur has become fully
self-aware of the people who should
be included in the visioning process
and how visioning meetings or retreats
should be structured for best results.   _____

The entrepreneur understands and
embraces the "No Year Two Allowed"
policy, understanding the reasons why it
improves visioning and planning.   _____

SIGNATURE: _____

DATE: _____

EXECUTION: GOALS AND ACCOUNTABILITY
AND KEY LEADERSHIP DECISION #1

"In the absence of clearly defined goals, we become strangely loyal to performing daily trivia until ultimately we become enslaved by it."

—ROBERT A. HEINLEIN

Ask an entrepreneur what's new, and you'll hear about product innovations, market expansions, new hires, and hard-won customers. I don't think I've ever heard somebody crowing, "I set up a new accountability system!" Entrepreneurs love to create companies and the new products and services that come with them. Entrepreneurs do *not* love to build accountability systems. But we should all love having them. Otherwise, how will our grand vision for the company get implemented? More importantly, **how will we ever scale our businesses for optimum growth without them?**

A SYSTEM IS A THING OF BEAUTY

Nobody sets out to be an *un*disciplined entrepreneur, of course. Everybody wants his or her company to run like a finely tuned machine. So, we CEOs pride ourselves on the quality of our bedside reading. We make time to attend seminars and workshops. But good intentions, and hours or dollars spent, only get us so far. Our success depends on our ability to implement what we learn, and that's where we too often fall short.

This difficulty we have with implementation is something I've already mentioned in this book, and it's a problem I think about quite a lot. In fact, what weaves the chapters of this book together is the challenge of implementation. I've seen with my own eyes the imbalance that exists between the motivation to learn and the motivation to do. I've watched many a colleague struggle with it. I've struggled, too.

Way back in 1999, I attended my first Birthing of Giants (BOG) program at the Massachusetts Institute of Technology. The program, which is now called the Entrepreneurial Masters Program (EMP), was developed for the Entrepreneurs' Organization by its founder, Verne Harnish. Verne's idea for BOG was to bring something of a master's-level program to a highly selective group of entrepreneurs from around the world who had founded and were running growth companies. Participation required a three-year commitment. My classmates and I met for a week each year at the MIT Endicott House in Boston, Massachusetts, to essentially drink from a fire hose of Verne's making. We were barraged with information and advice from some of the biggest names in entrepreneurial business, academia, and consulting. We learned about capital formation, marketing, innovation, organizational development—you name it, we got it, and in depth. In the first year alone, I took enough notes to fill three two-inch notebooks.

As fantastic as all this was, it was also mind-bogglingly disheartening to me. I had arrived at BOG confident that I was running a pretty nice little company. In fact, with year-to-year growth of over 50 percent for the eight previous years, we were practically the poster child for fast-growth business! But, by the time the first lunch break arrived on the first day, I'd already begun to realize that my "pretty nice little company" was actually highly inefficient. As hours turned into days in the classroom with my CEO colleagues and our business-world teachers, it was ironic to realize that what I didn't know about my business was coming at me so fast that I couldn't even get it all on paper. But, oh, how I tried. If there was ever a wake-up call or a first step toward my becoming a *Qualified* Entrepreneur, this was it.

I came home from the first BOG week all charged up and completely sold on entrepreneurial education. I signed up for more seminars. And, when Verne founded the consulting company Gazelles (a global executive education and coaching firm) and published a book that provided a how-to in many areas where my company was deficient, it became my go-to resource. The book is *Mastering the Rockefeller Habits: What You Must Do to Increase the Value of Your Fast-Growth Firm*, and in 2011 a *Wall Street Journal* survey of entrepreneurs ranked it among the top six self-help books to help them get their businesses off the ground or run them more smoothly. Verne recently published his highly anticipated revision, *Scaling Up: How a Few Companies Make It . . . and Why the Rest Don't (Rockefeller Habits 2.0)*. To this day, Verne's book (and more specifically, his *One-Page Strategic Plan*) are the springboard to success that I've used and continue to recommend. It provides a real understanding of why accountability is so important—and then it shows you how to develop the backbone of your company's own accountability system.

After some years of recommending Verne's book and his excellent seminars to peers, I started to notice something. Too many of us were seeing our efforts lose steam after a few supercharged months. **Reading the book or attending a seminar and coming home motivated—these are the easy parts. Maintaining the energy long enough to really affect change—well, that is much harder.** It takes a level of determination and, yes, discipline, that most companies and their CEOs find hard to maintain. I noticed that as the newness and excitement wore off, companies and their CEOs would find themselves pretty much back where they started, with one notable exception. Now, instead of committing readily to the CEO's change leadership, employees were likely to sit back skeptically and wait to see if the motivation from the top would last. After all, wasn't this just the flavor-of-the-month management strategy? Wasn't this likely to be another out-with-the-old-and-in-with-the-new exercise in futility? "Give it a few weeks," experience told many of these employees, "and it'll go away." The boss will be done with it and "on to something else."

Over time, it has become clear to me that when change loses steam in an organization, you are looking in the wrong direction if you look at middle management or employees or coaches. You need to look in the mirror—we all do, first and foremost.

ACCOUNTABILITY AND RESPONSIBILITY

"Vision without execution is hallucination!"
–THOMAS A. EDISON

Discipline starts at the top, plain and simple. Yes, we CEOs have to have a good strategic game plan, but it matters less what it is than that we stay doggedly committed to it. If we aren't committed and don't stay committed, how can we expect it of anyone else? There may be many ways to establish goals and accountability within an organization, but make no mistake, the pace aligns with the pulse at the top of the pyramid. It's the CEO who dictates the culture of accountability, or defaults to the lack of one. **Without discipline, without a game plan for accountability, an organization will never perform to its full capabilities—period and full stop.**

We often speak of military discipline (to name one type I know well), or the discipline insisted upon by an elementary school teacher in a classroom, or the discipline (rules and methods) of a church or religious order.[1] Often, those in authority who are establishing the discipline are seen negatively as people who dish out punishment. I prefer to think of the role as one where an individual *imposes order or a code of conduct.* Ideally, over time, discipline becomes a self-regulated activity within the organization:

> *Discipline is the assertion of willpower over more base desires, and is usually understood to be synonymous with self-control.*[2] *Self-discipline is to some extent a substitute for motivation, when one uses reason to determine the best course of action that opposes one's desires.*

"A substitute for motivation"—yes, to me, that's a nice way to think of it. In fact, I believe the definition works particularly well when talking about staying in good physical shape. There are many times when I don't want to run or lift weights, but my *discipline* takes over and, though the motivation may be clearly lacking, the workout happens entirely as a product of *self-control*. Is it so different running a business? I don't think so.

Let's face it, fellow entrepreneurs, our motivation lies far from the land of goals and measurement that make up an accountability discipline. Our motivation is to build growth companies. We crave autonomy and savor entrepreneurship because coming up with things to do or sell is creative and invigorating. Establishing accountability and structure? Not so much. It's hard work. It requires discipline, which is what needs to be in place if motivation isn't.

> There are many times when I don't want to run or lift weights, but my *discipline* takes over and, though the motivation may be clearly lacking, the workout happens entirely as a product of *self-control*. Is it so different running a business? I don't think so.

Of course, there are other options besides establishing an internal discipline to achieve goals. You can certainly substitute bare-knuckled authoritarian force, if that's how you want to get the job done, but that requires a level of micromanagement that we all know is bad for employees, companies, and CEOs alike. You can also practice avoidance and move lazily or energetically—your choice—among flavor-of-the-month strategies, never quite recognizing that what you're really doing is staying in motion to avoid recognizing how little you're actually doing. The worst part of that, as I've already mentioned, is what it does to employee buy-in. It doesn't take long before the workforce knows it can just wait you out, because there will always be another new idea or regimen coming.

Think back to a key part of the definition I gave you for *Disciplined* Entrepreneur (your first step in becoming a *Qualified* Entrepreneur):

- [He or she] becomes fully self-aware that, for the business to succeed long-term, a transition must occur from the business being about "me" as its entrepreneur/ CEO to the business being about the overall needs of the company.

It's really simple, then, isn't it? When your goal is making the best decision for the company and the entrepreneur, incorporating discipline—namely, accountability and structure—becomes a no-brainer for anyone who is serious about being a *Qualified* Entrepreneur. It's just necessary, part of the package.

Consider, too, how a lack of discipline impacts your role as leader. As I alluded to previously, it tends to make a CEO's job much harder. Either you're having to stay on top of your people at all times to ensure any progress gets made at all or you're put in the position of trying to figure out—without any real lens or benchmark—what's progress and what's not. So, in establishing a discipline for your company, I think one of the best questions you can ask to test the validity of one approach or another is: "Does this method have me judging success subjectively or objectively?" The right answer ought to be: *objectively*. The better and more specific the goal that is set, the more measurable it is, and the more easily you'll track progress toward achieving it.

Whenever you're faced with a goal that is general or subjective, you are forced to find ways of measuring progress that aren't clear and quantifiable. Often, it comes down to ambiguous questions such as how much effort someone is or isn't making. As CEO, the accountability discipline you establish for your organization should require that every goal be pegged to dates, names (who's accountable), and financial or otherwise-quantifiable results. Not all of these need to be reported directly to you as the CEO, but whatever the reporting structure you set up, the CEO should be the one providing clear, consistent leadership, top-down, to ensure the process works. Without that direction and oversight from you, your company is a football team without a game plan.

Of course, having an accountability discipline in place doesn't mean that the CEO is relieved of all management and is left free to think big thoughts. What it means is that he or she doesn't have to reach deeply into the organization to manage. Like a coach, *the CEO stays on the sidelines unless needed*—to provide additional information, to offer encouragement, or to call a halt on things that aren't being corrected quickly enough. There is no yelling or micromanaging. With a discipline in place that is top-down, the communication can and should be bottom-up.

MAKE YOUR ACCOUNTABILITY LEADERSHIP DECISION: CEO- OR COO-LED?

It's true that you do not need to make the all-important Second Decision until the end of this book. But you need to make a preliminary and highly significant judgment—one of your biggest as *Qualified* Entrepreneur—right now: **When it comes to systems, goals, and accountability, will you as CEO be the driver of discipline and execution in your organization? Or will that responsibility rest with a COO or other type of Operations leader?**

Here's a pertinent passage from the definition of *Disciplined* Entrepreneur:

> [He or she] commits to undertaking the preparation necessary for making the Second Decision. **This is a conscious choice to acquire a more disciplined approach to management and leadership—or to bring that discipline to the company in another way.** The Disciplined Entrepreneur knows that it's less important how his or her role is shaped than that the company excels and succeeds.

What I'm presenting isn't really an either-or decision—your company needs the skill set of a COO as much as it does a CEO, regardless of who's doing each or whether one person attempts to do both. The answer you provide to the CEO/COO question in the context of execution and accountability depends on how you function right now, so take titles out of the equation. Do you function as the visionary for the company, or as the operational excellence person? Surely there's somebody out there who can fulfill both roles with aplomb, but it's rare that both hats fit the same head at the same time. So which is the best fit for you? For examples, think Apple (Steve Jobs/Tim Cook) and Facebook (Mark Zuckerberg/Sheryl Sandberg).

To think more deeply about which role fits you best, try to zero in on what you're most passionate about. As we all know, there's a big difference between "I can do that" and "I love to do that." There have been many times in my career when I was good at my job, but not particularly enthusiastic about it. In the US Navy, I was an engineer and a pretty good one, but I felt I'd really arrived at my destination when I became an "Officer of the Deck," certified to drive a submarine. Similarly, in business, there were times that I functioned well as a COO, but I always knew that my true calling was to be a CEO—and, eventually, a *Qualified* Entrepreneur in that role.

In my nearly 25 years in the entrepreneurial community, and more specifically in my 10-plus years membership in both EO and Vistage, I can pinpoint the lack of an A+ Operations leader as one of the most consistent leadership mistakes an entrepreneurial CEO makes in their growth organization.

My guess is that most of you are, like me, better at laying out plans and strategies than executing them. Obviously, execution is crucial for organizations if they are to improve, move forward, and grow. Consistent feedback has to be in place, and progress needs to be measured. Who does that in your company? If you have been the one putting plans and processes into place, then who follows up and tracks outcomes? If, like so many of us, you are great at strategizing and implementing and horrible at following up, you'll watch each quarter go by without a lot of accomplishment—just a revolving door of new plans and goals, and a company continually suffering from a bad case of "set it and forget it."

Whether you have somebody with the title of COO or Operations Manager or something else is immaterial—I'll leave the labels to you. What does matter is whether your organization has operational discipline, and that's on you. You need to be the one determining how to fill the operational gaps, if you have them. And I'll bet you do.

To be more certain of which side of the fence you're on, ask yourself:

- If there is some sort of "fire" to put out and a strategic session to lead, both demanding your time, which would you more eagerly do?

- If you are worried about the company meeting its quarterly goal, do you dive in and figure out what combination of increased revenue and decreased expenses will get you back on track, or do you delegate those decisions so that you can focus on the longer-term initiatives that will avoid the issue next year? Another way to ask the same question—do you spend time ensuring your staff is trained and competent to handle the end-of-quarter results, or do you jump in and do it for them?

- If you have people issues to resolve, how often do they lure you in or default to you? As long as all the "important and immediate" issues in your company require your presence, input, and problem-solving skills, you will have ever greater difficulty finding time to fulfill the strategic requirements of being CEO.

This is going to sound like a chapter-ending tribute, and it is, but I hope it's also a helpful example of shared leadership with separate roles: I was blessed to be half of a CEO-COO duo for almost two decades. My COO L.J. Hirnikel was career Army before starting his entrepreneurial career with me in 1994, and I'm proud to call him my business partner and friend. We understood each other's strengths and weaknesses, and where skill sets were concerned, his came in where mine left off—and vice versa. Sure, we had our disagreements, but always for the purpose of bettering the company. Even when the discussion went long and got heated, we always managed to settle the beef and go right back to work. "Twenty years, where'd they go?" sings guitarist Bob Seger in the 1980s hit "Like a Rock." As is the case in any long relationship, L.J. and I worked well together for two decades because we made each other better. I couldn't imagine expanding my role to include his, and I know for a fact that L.J. would have wondered what the problem was had I given him any of my CEO duties. He wanted to work *in* the business—and that's what allowed me to work *on* the business. We also had complete trust in one another, which allowed us to focus on our own jobs with both autonomy and accountability. I know I speak for L.J. when I say this: **if you're trying to be both CEO and COO, one of your roles is getting neglected.** It's up to you to recognize which role that is, and take action to provide your company someone who brings not just skills but passion to those duties.

As we leave the Vision and Execution chapters, I want to highlight a couple of the top 10 reasons such a high percentage of small businesses are out of business by Years 5 and 10:[3]

- **Operational mediocrity:** Often the problem is being unwilling or unable to terminate non-performers and get the right people in the right seat. (In the case of the Second Decision, the only person I am asking you to evaluate in this regard is yourself.)

- **Dysfunctional management:** Not enough focus, vision, planning, standards, and other requirements of good management.

CHAPTER 6 QUAL CARD

Initial each requirement as met:

PREREQUISITES	INITIALS
The entrepreneur has committed to establishing discipline, starting by choosing and implementing an accountability and execution system for their organization and completing the *One-Page Strategic Plan*, putting a copy in the QE Notebook.	_____
The entrepreneur fully accepts his/her own accountability leadership responsibilities, absolving employees and direct reports of fault until disciplined thinking is embraced at the CEO level.	_____
The entrepreneur has committed to establishing discipline, starting with making the key leadership decision of who will own the execution/accountability system—the CEO or the COO/Operations leader.	_____
The entrepreneur fully understands that discipline is synonymous with self-control and to some extent a substitute for motivation.	_____

SIGNATURE: _____

DATE: _____

SIX MONTHS' CASH AND COVENANTS

AND KEY LEADERSHIP DECISION #2

"What gets measured gets managed."

—ATTRIBUTED TO PETER DRUCKER

As the old saying goes, cash is king. You want to grow? It takes cash. You want to hire people, open offices, add inventory, buy supplies, or pay rent? Everything you do requires cash. But do you really know at any given moment whether you are cash-rich or cash-poor? Can you portray your cash position with data, or do you resort to generalities or even hope?

If you're hemming and hawing instead of answering, you aren't alone. What we all need to ask ourselves is, how can something so important take a backseat—ever?

Lack of cash makes every top 5 or top 10 list of why small businesses fail. Year after year, even some of the most reputable and well-respected fast-growth companies fall victim to a crisis of liquidity.

Some sources estimate that 60 percent, or even up to 90 percent of small business failures owe their demise to lack of cash or poor cash flow.[1,2]

What's going on? All I can assume is that too many of us understand the issue only at a superficial level—or that we're just plain unwilling to do what it takes to really preserve cash. Or perhaps it's just another sad symptom of the entrepreneurial urge run amok—we catch the growth virus and live with it until it kills us. Whatever the reason, operating with a lack of cash is—as my close friend and business partner Bill Laughlin, former P-3 pilot in the US Navy, would put it—"like flying blind." Would it surprise you to know that another top reason for failures is out-of-control growth?[3] This would include over-expansion and borrowing too much money in an attempt to keep growth at a particular rate. Sometimes less is more!

> Would it surprise you to know that another top reason for failures is out-of-control growth? This would include over-expansion and borrowing too much money in an attempt to keep growth at a particular rate. Sometimes less is more!

If each of us is to become a *Qualified* Entrepreneur, we need to acquire a deep understanding of the importance of liquidity. We need to maintain a firm grasp on what it takes to keep cash in the business, and we need to walk the talk—daily. For the past 20 years, checking my company's cash position has been an everyday task for me, and I know that it has been the single most important factor in keeping my companies solvent and growing sensibly. It's nothing very complicated; just a simple comparison of cash in to cash out. It should be *your* daily task, too. This chapter will give you not only the tool you need, but also the reasoning behind why you're the one and only person in your organization that can make best use of it.

It all boils down to a new and more specific cash slogan:

Six months' cash is the new king.

Yes, I mean exactly what that says. I want you to know what your cash balance is each day, and be able to project what that balance will be each month thereafter to a minimum of six months out. Why? Because cash plots a different trend line than growth. When you are growing and sales are rising every month, along with your expenses, cash is the metric that lags. You're always spending your money on expenses before you're being paid for your sales. As long as expenses grow, cash will continue to lag. You may have money in the bank today, and that's great. I'm glad you're tracking that. But what's your balance going to be six months from today? What if this is just the peak of the cash trend, and worse days are ahead? That's where your focus needs to be: a full six months ahead. **I want you to recalculate your six-month projected cash balance on the first day of every month (at a minimum), so that there is never a time when you are flying blind.** I want you to be able to understand and visualize not just your organization's cash *position,* but also be able to understand and visualize your company's cash *trends.*

DANGER AHEAD!

I know that tracking cash isn't a new concept. Many of you may feel you're already doing a decent job of knowing how much cash you've got on hand via the cash-flow statements that are generated with your other financial statements. If your business is still on a cash basis for accounting, you may be getting what you need from a traditional cash-flow statement. It shows you what cash you have on hand, at least for the short term. But most of us operate businesses that are big enough and complicated enough to report on an accrual basis. (Banks tend to insist on it.) And we who use accrual accounting are the ones most in need of a better process for tracking cash. Here's why: **the difference between having cash on hand and making profit on an accrual basis is a danger zone—one that has the potential to put us out of business, if we're not careful.** Even when sales are booming? Yes, even when sales are booming—*especially* when sales are booming.

So, let's get down to the nitty-gritty of tracking a cash trend. Suppose it's January 1, and I have $400,000 in cash in the business, plus a $1 million line of credit. Sweet! I have $1.4 million with which to grow my business, right? Wrong. First, a $1 million line of credit isn't worth a million; in my case, it's worth a percentage of accounts receivable, because banks are smart and want to reduce their risk exposure. So, in my example, I can only tap the line of credit for $700,000. That's disappointing, but still not much of a concern, because sales are growing each month. Let's look at what my six-month cash analysis shows:

Date	Cash Balance	Month Expenses	Accounts Receivable	Projected Collections	Cash +/-	Sales	Profit/Loss	Available Credit Line Balance ($700,000)
1/1	400,000	1,000,000	2,500,000	750,000	250,000	1,000,000	0	700,000
2/1	150,000	1,050,000	2,750,000	825,000	225,000	1,100,000	50,000	700,000
3/1	75,000	1,050,000	3,025,000	825,000	225,000	1,100,000	50,000	625,000
4/1	300,000	1,100,000	3,375,000	950,000	150,000	1,300,000	200,000	400,000
5/1	450,000	1,100,000	3,575,000	1,000,000	150,000	1,200,000	100,000	250,000
6/1	600,000	1,150,000	3,775,000	1,100,000	50,000	1,300,000	150,000	100,000
7/1	650,000	1,150,000	3,875,000	1,250,000	100,000	1,350,000	200,000	50,000
8/1	550,000	1,150,000	4,025,000	1,250,000	100,000	1,400,000	250,000	150,000
9/1	450,000	1,200,000	4,025,000	1,350,000	150,000	1,350,000	150,000	250,000
10/1	300,000	1,200,000	4,025,000	1,400,000	200,000	1,400,000	200,000	400,000

Notice that my growth in sales and profits are both absolutely outstanding. Behind the numbers we obviously have an organization that is firing on all cylinders—we can assume that morale is high, people are performing, and new leaders are being identified and promoted. Everything I promised my people about growth, wealth, and opportunity would seem to be coming true. If this isn't living the dream, what is?

But, my expenses are growing too, mostly because I've had to keep hiring to keep up with my sales growth. In fact, it's hard to add enough people to keep up with market demand. Luckily, my company is doing so well that folks are clamoring for the opportunity to join the organization. They're good people, too—my employees are referring great prospects left and right.

Even with the added expense of increased employment, the figures look pretty good. Accounts receivable increases almost daily, and collections are going up. (Not to get ahead of myself here, since metrics are two chapters ahead of us, but DSO—days sales outstanding—is a great way of detecting weakness in your collections process, and yes, it's a an extremely important metric to track. DSO measures the average number of days that a company takes to collect revenue after a sale has been made.)

With that useful digression behind us, let's further zero in on what's happening to cash in the above chart: by July 1, I'll be at −$650,000 (yep—red numbers are negative numbers), leaving me only $50,000 available on the credit line. That and that alone is the woefully thin line separating my business from paying its bills or not paying its bills. Wow. I need cash.

If my wallet is a little thin, I can go to an ATM. If I've got a generous investor, I might be able to talk him or her into providing a bit more investment. If I have partners, we can ante up more of our own money. Those of you with venture capital are playing a game I haven't played and don't understand, so I can't comment on how you get more money from a VC. But for most of us, that line of credit is the best shot we've got. When it's gone, it's gone.

This is why it's so important to be continually projecting and understanding your cash trend six months into the future. You can't make decisions on your gut. You have to know, on paper, that you really will have the cash you need when you need it. You must be certain that the opportunities you're chasing aren't going to end up killing you. And if you want an especially great reason to pay better attention to cash, it's this: you'll sleep better. Simply by tracking your cash burn, you'll likely avoid the tremendous stress of wondering whether you'll meet payroll or not. That, I can say with assurance, is a benefit that easily validates the entire exercise of projecting cash.

Here I'll reveal that the example shown above in the six-month table isn't hypothetical. I've lived it many times and, twice in my career, I experienced major episodes of it. The first time, in 1998, it nearly killed my company. The second time, in 2004, I used my six-month cash projection to plan my way around the impending disaster—and I've continued to do so many times since.

The year 1998 was a banner year in my life—I'd remarried, created a *Brady Bunch*-style blended family of four girls and two boys, ages 4-13, and my business was experiencing off-the-charts growth. Motivated by sheer opportunity that year, we had decided to open up six new offices in six months. This was the moment I mentioned earlier when my wife asked me, "Do you know what you're doing?" It stopped me cold, but I answered "Yes, and I'm completely offended, I might add." In hindsight, years later, I can admit that it was at best a half-truth though, *because I didn't know what I didn't know.* I was tracking cash, but not *six months' cash* as a *Qualified* Entrepreneur must do.

Lo and behold, by August 1998, our company looked something like the example in the six-month cash analysis table. In the midst of what should have been a wonderful family beach vacation, I found myself on the phone begging the bank to extend our credit line so we could make payroll. When the bank resisted, I became indignant. What good is having a million dollar credit line if you can't access it? It was then I learned that the bank didn't consider my accounts receivable high enough to warrant the entire million. It was also then that I was reminded once again of what a line of credit is for: handling short-term cash-flow fluctuations. It's not to fund operations. It's not a get-out-of-jail-free card.

What an eye-opener that was. Here we were at the brightest moment in our company's history, yet it was also our darkest. Sales were booming, profits too, yet here I was, worrying about making payroll—and wondering if my company would be just the latest example of a fast-growth company killed by cash. It was by no means a carefree beach vacation for me, not that year. But with the help of the credit line—and many, many calls to the bank to explain the why's of our predicament and the how's of what I was doing to fix it—the company weathered the crisis.

When the dust settled, I vowed I'd never get blindsided by cash burn again. From that time forward, I committed to calculating at least six months of cash projections on the first day of every month. Here's the simple model I've used ever since that first cash crisis:

Cash balance + Projected monthly collections – Monthly cash expenses = Growth decisions

This, my friends, is the single most important monthly calculation that we, as *Qualified* Entrepreneurs, need in front of us when making decisions to spend money. With this data in hand, you simply can't get sucked into a bad deal. If the new business you're considering requires two new employees, and you can see that the expense will bring you to a negative cash position in six months or less, you now have some real data with which to ask yourself, is it worth it and can we fund it? If you anticipate decreased collections for some reason, the model will confirm that you can't take on the additional expense. If you're convinced that the new opportunity you're considering is risky but important, you will be able to very quickly determine that the only way forward is via increased investment or an expanded line of credit—and the model will give you the lead time you need to pursue your options.

> Cash balance + Projected monthly collections – Monthly cash expenses = Growth decisions

That's exactly what happened in my business in 2004. In January of that year, I alerted my business partners that we would have to put more money into the business. Without the infusion, our growing company would burn through its cash before summer, I told them. Their response was less than enthusiastic until I showed them the facts—ones very similar to those you saw in the six-month cash analysis table. The bank, on the other hand, was immediately receptive and very appreciative. Remember, bankers are conservative and want their money back. Not only did my detailed cash projections give them confidence in my ability to proactively run the business, but they also found it impressive that my partners and I believed enough in the company to reinvest from our personal funds. I'm convinced that giving our lenders an increased level of comfort always pays dividends, and this episode certainly solidified the banking relationship for our company. The bank flexed for us whenever it could, and when we renewed our line of credit, it was on better terms.

The six-month cash analysis table should be sufficient to guide you (or your financial person) in coming up with a cash forecast that works for you and your business. Simply project your revenues, expenses, and collections for each month going forward, and you'll easily have a projected bank balance with which to making spending decisions. You certainly don't need a CFO for this, and you probably don't have one anyway. An accountant or a book-keeper can easily set you up with what you need. (I have the model built on my website to assist in this process.

But I want to offer you two cautions. First, make sure that whoever prepares the data understands that you want realistic or even conservative numbers. Yes, it's fun to look at optimistic numbers and get excited about how great things are going—and if you really need to do this, why not keep a separate set of numbers just for positive reinforcement? But for good decision making, it's the realistic-to-worst-case-scenario numbers you want to be looking at. They're the figures that will help you wear the special badge of honor we entrepreneurs all yearn to earn—the one for never failing to make payroll! Where decisions that affect cash are concerned, you don't want to guess and hope. You want to gather data and know.

My second caution relates to the lure of expedience, otherwise known as managerial laziness. Don't think you can offload the accountability for cash to somebody in your financial zone, perhaps in the interest of efficiency or to "keep the responsibility where the expertise is." Tracking cash trends needs to be *your* continuing project as CEO. You are the leader who sets the vision and makes the growth decisions for your business, right? And cash is a major factor as you try to execute your vision, right? Then yours need to be the eyes on the cash statement. Relying on anyone else is a huge and potentially fatal mistake. Here's why: no one in your organization has the motivation that you do, to not only look at these numbers, but really *see* them. Again, it's about growing the business and making payroll. Nobody who works for you sees the faces of the

> First, make sure that whoever prepares the data understands that you want realistic or even conservative numbers. They're the figures that will help you wear the special badge of honor we entrepreneurs all yearn to earn—the one for never failing to make payroll!

workforce the way you do. Nobody else feels the responsibility of holding so many lives and aspirations in their hands. These truths make you the most motivated person in the organization when it comes to using cash projections to make good decisions. Nobody else can even hope to understand the responsibility in the same way.

Come to think of it, there's another aspect of this. Unless you're a much better negotiator than I am, you have signed numerous personal guarantees over the years, just to open or enlarge a bank's line of credit. Think of the times you slid a piece of paper across the kitchen table for your wife's (or husband's) signature, saying, "It's for the bank, but don't worry, they'll never get the house." Well, ignoring your six-month cash position could make you a liar in a hurry! Why would you even consider delegating a function so important as projecting cash when you are so personally and pro-fessionally liable for the decisions you make with—or without—it?

> **Think of the times you slid a piece of paper across the kitchen table for your wife's (or husband's) signature, saying, "It's for the bank, but don't worry, they'll never get the house." Well, ignoring your six-month cash position could make you a liar in a hurry!**

THE IMPORTANT ROLE OF COVENANTS

Since I've raised the issue of personal guarantees, let's segue to the second half of this chapter's title and talk about covenants. Unless you're one of the rare business people who can self-fund his or her business from a big wad of personal cash (hey, good for you or them!) you're reliant on a lender—a banker, a financier, or somebody else who's letting you borrow money on terms. Financial covenants are what protect the lender, ensuring timely repayment of the loan by the guarantor (you) and providing the person with the deep pockets some peace of mind.

Each set of financial covenants differs in its own way, because each lender-guarantor relationship is different. But typical covenants include:

- A maximum credit line—a ceiling on the amount of cash to be loaned in a period of time.

- Credit line calculations that restrict the total amount to be loaned. A typical example would be for the lender to loan based on a percentage of overall accounts receivable (70–90 percent is common, but the amount depends on your relationship with the lender).

- Leverage ratios—the total amount of debt/trailing 12 months' EBITDA (Earnings Before Interest, Taxes, Depreciation, and Amortization).

- Limits on capital expenditures.

- Minimum levels for trailing 12 months' EBITDA.

Looking at this list, it occurs to me that maybe **the new king is six months' cash *and* covenants!** It's a better name, because I also want you to extend out your covenant calculations to at least six months. Just as it's important to be able to see and forecast cash trends, it's equally important to see and forecast how your business's trends are affecting your covenants. Are you bumping up against some limits or requirements, maybe creeping out of compliance? That's not a small issue. Your lender is likely to prevent you from investing in the business until those numbers are back in the acceptable range. And having cash on hand to spend but no ability spend it is, well, a bummer.

So what you're really managing against, when you carry debt in a growing business, are two potential financial crises, both of which can only occur if you take your eye off the financial ball:

Crisis 1: You run out of cash internally and exceed your current credit limits, effectively putting all business spending on hold until you can resolve things.

Crisis 2: You violate your financial covenants and your lender (a) restricts your financial operations until you can get your covenants back into an acceptable range, (b) forces you to renegotiate your terms, which a betting man would say results in higher interest or punitive terms, or, in the worst case, (c) calls in your loan balance and makes you figure out how to pay it. None of these is desirable, of course, and the mere threat of even getting close to one of these consequences should be all the encouragement you need to keep your eye on the ball.

It's another example of what I talk so much about in this book: CEOs of the entrepreneurial type may prefer to spend money without regard to the details of managing it, but there comes a point in your career where such an attitude is plain irresponsible. If you're reading this book, I think that *you* think you're there. So delegate the gathering of data if you wish, but never fool yourself into thinking you can delegate the accountability. Risk may have been your calling card as an entrepreneur for a long time, and maybe it's your preferred mode of operation. But discipline is what it takes to preserve what you've built and grow it to the next level.

As you think about improving your approach to tracking cash and financial covenants, don't forget to factor in your entrepreneurial personality. **Ever Optimistic** believes that everything is fine, so there is a real possibility that he or she won't track cash to the level of detail necessary to manage a growing business. **Reflexively Pessimistic** can't help but worry, and so will probably know to two decimal points where cash stands—and what expenses or investments need to be conservatively managed to protect it. If you tend to be **Urgent/Reactive**, you will have to learn to quit letting things get to the point of disaster and start planning ahead—because there is no fire extinguisher big enough or fast enough to put out the blaze caused by an untimely shortage of cash.

> **Ever Optimistic** believes that everything is fine, so there is a real possibility that he or she won't track cash to the level of detail necessary to manage a growing business.

The *Qualified* Entrepreneur—the one who is striving to become a **Steady/Proactive** leader—*commits* to becoming ever more self-aware, with the aim of increasing the fact-based rigor underlying his or her business decisions. Six months' cash and covenants *are* king to Steady/Proactive. He or she recognizes these financial trends as the lifeblood of the business, in fact. So, be Steady/Proactive and play it smart! When it comes to being able to pay your employees each month, that's not a game that anyone wants to lose. Track at least six months' cash, and recalculate the projection at least monthly to truly understand the trend. Know your financial covenants and whether you're about to violate them. **Another top 10 failure list entrant is poor accounting; you cannot be in control of your business if you don't know what is really going on, financially speaking.[4] Don't let your business become another failure statistic.**

LEADERSHIP DECISION—ACCOUNTING MANAGER OR CFO?

Just as you made a CEO/COO decision a chapter ago, you now have an equally important leadership decision to make in your growing organization: How will you get the financial reporting, analysis, and decision making your business needs? Who will produce the cash statements, the calculations to check against your financial covenants, and additional reports (such as those we'll talk about in the next two chapters)? Who will interpret these reports? If yours is a larger company, perhaps greater than $10 million in annual revenue, you may already employ a CFO. The more complex your financial setup, the more you need a CFO. (One of my friends in the venture capital world had a CFO very early in the game for this exact reason—complexity.) CFOs are much less common in smaller companies, however, and I'd say that's as it should be. CFOs aren't cheap hires. During the fast-growth years, it's usually much more economical for most entrepreneurs to contract with a CPA at a local accounting firm than to add a financial executive to the mix.

My observation is that many entrepreneurs call their financial manager a CFO, but in reality the position functions more like an accounting manager, an accountant, or a CFO. In my opinion, a rose by any other name smells as sweet. All you really need in early-phase growth is an expert in debits and credits—somebody who, internally or externally, produces monthly statements and, given enough bandwidth, also handles vendor contracts and produces monthly statements, as my accounting manager did. As your business continues to grow, though, you will need someone who can produce critical reports and generate metrics beyond the normal end-of-the-month financial statements, because, as we've just discussed, cash alone threatens to put you out of business.

My first business used an external accountant who would take our books each month and hand them back to us with a balance sheet, an income statement, and a cash flow statement. He also did the paperwork necessary to file taxes, and because we were an S-corporation, he gave us our K-1s so we could add our business contributions to our individual tax returns. As we grew, we needed additional expertise to handle business in multiple states, so we switched to a mid-level accounting firm that was capable of giving us much more in-depth guidance. In addition, we hired accounting staff to take care of the internal financial work that needed to be done each month.

Eventually, we grew large enough to hire an accounting manager who was responsible for the entire financial department. We still had our taxes done by an independent CPA, though, and we never did get to the point of hiring a CFO. Why? Because I was able to fulfill part of that financial role. Whereas engineering came hard to me, I was an accounting major in college and numbers were easy for me. I also enjoy working with numbers; so in my businesses, I was the one who developed systems and financial metrics to help us track and scale the business. The reports eventually came from my staff in Finance, but in the end, I functioned as a CEO/CFO. I developed the reports I wanted and analyzed the financial information within them to help us grow.

But talking to other CEOs for many years tells me that this is another area, like Operations, where too many leaders punt. Either they outsource the financial reporting and analysis to their accounting manager, openly expressing bewilderment or hostility regarding "the financial stuff," or they give themselves the role, order up monthly reports—and give them much less focus than they really need to.

While it makes sense to put off hiring a CFO, it's dangerous to assume that a CEO can wear the hat long-term. If the CEO is uncomfortable with numbers and punts, it can leave the company very exposed. Just because your accounting manager can run the department flawlessly and get the reports out accurately and on time doesn't mean that he or she can become capable of CFO-level thinking and analysis. To help you make your decision for your organization moving forward and for your Qual Card, I offer up the following definitions for you to consider.

Accounting Manager Job Description

The accounting manager uses professional accounting concepts and internal company policies to solve complex accounting issues, including the maintenance of internal controls. Participates in and implements monthly financial close, supervises the assignments of the staff accountants to include general ledger, accounts payable, and fixed assets. Prepares monthly management financial reporting package and executive summary schedules. Coordinates and facilitates the process of documenting accounting policies and procedures.[5]

Chief Financial Officer Job Description

A chief financial officer manages an organization's financial operations and risks. This is achieved by supervising accounting and finance staff, establishing accounting and finance policies and procedures for the company, and establishing and maintaining budgets, credit, and cash flows. Chief financial officer job descriptions can follow general job description formats, but must have specific management and finance items listed in essential functions, education, skills, and experience.[6]

These job descriptions depict two very different animals—as different as COOs are from CEOs, in fact. Every company needs financial analysis and financial reporting. The role traditionally played by a CFO involves managing risk. It's an important role that almost never should be played by someone with an accounting manager's skills and outlook. If you can't afford a CFO, the onus is on you as CEO to figure out how that key slot will be filled. Is it yours to take on? Or do you need to farm it out to an outside financial guru who possesses the skills to think beyond the spreadsheet?

CHAPTER 7 QUAL CARD

Initial each requirement as met:

PREREQUISITES

The entrepreneur has become fully
self-aware of his/her personality type
in relation to managing cash (Urgent/
Reactive, Ever Optimistic, Reflexively Pessimistic, or Steady/Proactive).   _____

The entrepreneur has developed a regimen
for forecasting cash needs monthly and
at least six months in advance, and is
receiving a daily cash report.   _____

The entrepreneur has developed a regimen
for forecasting the organization's financial
covenants at least six months in advance
to predict and prevent breaches.   _____

After personally reviewing the new Six
Months' Cash and Covenants forecast
each month, the entrepreneur has made
it a practice to compare the next quarter's
goals with the forecast to ensure there
are no glaring conflicts between goals,
availability of cash, and the ability to
stay in acceptable range of the business's
financial covenants. This review is done
with full regard to the capital expenditures (personnel, equipment, etc.) that are
planned but not yet made.   _____

The entrepreneur has made the CFO/
accounting manager decision, thus
ensuring that a designated financial
position exists to either assist or lead the
task of tracking cash in the business. _____

The entrepreneur has added to the QE
Notebook three items: the signed personal
guarantee forms from the bank and up-
to-date Six Months' Cash and Covenants
forecasts. _____

SIGNATURE: _____

DATE: _____

COGS-NIZANCE: PROFIT AND EXPENSE LEADERSHIP

"Life is like a ten-speed bicycle. Most of us have gears we never use."

—CHARLES SCHULTZ

What is "COGS-nizance"? It's your knowledge of your COGS—cost of goods sold. Think for a moment about your monthly financial statements—specifically, *you* and your financial statements. How do you interact with them?

- Which of the statements that you receive attracts your attention first? Second? Third?

- Do you read your financial statements from top to bottom and left to right, or do you skip to the bottom line? If you're bottom-line oriented, do you then go back and read the whole statement? Or are you like an impatient mystery-reader who only cares about the last page, where both the crime and the culprit are revealed?

- Are you the kind of financial-statement consumer who cares only about profit, comparing this year to last year—either in raw numbers or percentages? Or are you deeply into the details, checking to see if the targets you set were hit, indicating that improvements were made in efficiency, productivity, and cost-effectiveness?

- Then there is the question that must be asked: Are you punting on all of this? Are you leaving all of this financial statements stuff to somebody else—a bookkeeper, an outside accountant, your accounting manager, or a CFO?

That last question separates the noobs and wannabes from the entrepreneurs with lots of signatures on his or her Qual Card. It's kind of like the seawater question I've been asking you, the one the Captain asked me in my US Navy career: How does a drop of seawater power the light over your bunk? Imagine your own navy-style check-out with higher-ups: Suppose *your* captain—which, in your case may be your board of directors, your investors, or a trusted mentor—sits you down and asks you to explain how a dollar of revenue becomes profit in your enterprise. You'd be required to explain the breakdown of every dollar spent in your business to net a profit—your *cost of goods sold* (COGS). Could you do it? Would you walk away with your Qual Card signed off? (Excerpts from my actual US Navy Qual Cards are in Appendix D.)

The term COGS isn't unfamiliar, I'm sure. But for clarity's sake, let me state that for purpose of this discussion I'm defining COGS as all expenses in your business, in terms of percent of revenue, or at times, cents on the dollar. **The point is profit, and the key**

question is: What are you spending to create profit? You can customize your COGS measurements however your industry (and GAAP) dictates. But you need to understand the impact of *all* of your expenses—not just some of them, and not just the major categories of expense.

Now, back to the check-out question from your "captain" above. If your only answer to the profit question is that selling more stuff or serving more customers means making more money, you shouldn't be driving the submarine quite yet. You don't understand it well enough. Or, better put, you haven't applied enough *discipline*—yet—to your understanding of profit.

Boosting profit by increasing sales revenue is a great strategy for when times are good and the game is all offense. Entrepreneurs are naturals in this sort of game, because they are built to strive for more and more. But if the go-go environment is all you've ever known and riding the wave forward with it is the only strategy you understand, well, you're not ready to command the ship. Eventually the situation will become more adverse and defensive tactics will be required.

WHY COGS NUMBERS AND PERCENTAGES ARE YOUR BUSINESS'S CRITICALLY IMPORTANT NUMBERS

So you need to get cozy with, and thoroughly cognizant of, your COGS. How do you do this? By maintaining a rolling three-year COGS report that tells you not just the actual numbers, but also the percentage of your revenue that you're spending on every expense in your business—especially payroll COGS.

I'm not advocating that you bury yourself under paperwork or launch a major financial reconnaissance mission. You can get the data quickly and easily from one spreadsheet on one piece of paper—your end-of-year income statement. With this easily derived data set, you can answer that hypothetical question from your "captain," whoever she, he, or they may be. You'll readily know how many cents of every dollar of revenue you're spending on sales, marketing, payroll, utilities, etc.

> You need to get cozy with, and thoroughly cognizant of, your COGS.

This is one situation in which having a percentage is actually more helpful than having numbers. As I've told many an entrepreneur, having numbers gets you started, but it's only part of the analysis that's necessary. (In fact, those raw numbers can be misleading.) You also need the percentages—the relative weight of the COGS in one area of your business compared with the others you track. It provides you, as CEO, with what I consider to be the Big Picture for your operation.

Tracking COGS allows you to simplify the monitoring of your costs and, better yet, to add a crucial forward focus to your decision making. *That's because COGS percentages allow you to make apples-to-apples comparisons of your business, regardless of the differences in revenue from year to year.* It gives you a macro perspective on where you can spend more money and where you need to spend less to ensure consistent profit as revenue fluctuates. By focusing on COGS, you're not lost on a trend line plotted with actual numbers.

You're looking at a constant percentage that you've set as a goal for each category of expenditure, and that makes it easy: you simply adjust your strategy as you see the percentage ebb or flow.

Suppose the economy suddenly tanks, or your competitor comes out with a new product that steals some of your market share, or you lose some key personnel, or you become a defendant in a lawsuit. Any one of these things—and many others—can steal your focus to the extent that they threaten your company's performance. You may not believe it can happen to you, but it can and probably will. The pleasure cruise always runs the risk of rougher seas, and, each year, even some of the companies with the greatest strength, experience, and navigation skills

That's because COGS percentages allow you to make apples-to-apples comparisons of your business, regardless of the differences in revenue from year to year.

will be forced into port. Look at any past year's list of Fortune 500 or Inc. 500 companies, then fast-forward a few years and see if there aren't at least a few names missing. It's hard to separate the sold, merged, and renamed companies from those that suffered a reduced growth rate, a loss of revenue, or, worse, bankruptcy or liquidation. But they're there. Each year, bad things happen to good companies and some are unable to recover. Maybe the problem was cash. But it's equally possible that COGS is the factor they overlooked, creating that cash problem. Controlling

COGS is, like cash, one of the key things that can keep your company from being one of those sad stories we read about in the business pages.

Many struggling companies haven't figured out how to control expenses.[1] This shortcoming, similar to the lack of a cash cushion, makes most top 10 lists of reasons that companies fail at the 5- and 10-year point (or underperform with reduced profits). Also on most lists is when a company's math simply doesn't work—there's not enough demand for their product or service at a price that will produce a profit. We can and must do better at understanding our numbers!

Being a rubber-meets-the-road kind of guy, I now want to build you an example of how failure creeps up on a company. (This example is 100 percent real, though the numbers used are not.)

Orion, my first business, was really rolling in the late 1990s; it was posting year-over-year increases in both revenue and profitability. In 2001, as we all know, our nation suffered the terrorist attacks of 9/11, and the economy took a huge hit soon after. Like many companies, we were forced to downsize. Given the rapid drop in inquiries and sales, management knew that there was no choice but to reduce expenses by over $3 million in barely two years. That meant layoffs, large and painful layoffs, yet it still wasn't enough. The red ink kept flowing. In fact, it was so bad that had we not learned how to manage cash, we probably would have been out of business in a matter of months.

Why was the reduction in expenses not stemming the red ink? Because I was focusing on numbers alone, that's why. I was not paying attention to the percentage of revenue that payroll was costing the business, and COGS-Payroll was responsible for the bleeding. In the example table, you can see that the percentage of sales spent on payroll rose from 50 percent to 79 percent in one year, which, defined another way, represented a 29 percent hit to the company's profitability. *That's why, even though we had conducted layoffs and, by 2002, reduced payroll by almost $3 million, we were still losing money!*

	Sales	Payroll	Payroll COGS %	Profit %
1998	8,500,000	5,100,000	60%	15%
1999	11,000,000	6,050,000	55%	20%
2000	12,000,000	6,000,000	50%	25%
2001	7,000,000	5,500,000	79%	-15%
2002	4,000,000	3,000,000	75%	-5%
2003	3,500,000	2,450,000	70%	0%
2004	5,000,000	3,250,000	65%	5%

We often say that "the numbers tell the story." Well, where COGS is concerned, the percentages are what help to tell the *whole* story. Honestly, in my experience, there is no better way of monitoring the health of your business—quickly, easily, and without having

We often say that "the numbers tell the story." Well, where COGS is concerned, the percentages are what help to tell the *whole* story.

to decipher lots of actual numbers to get to your analysis—than with COGS percentages. Watching your COGS percentages is like watching body temperature rise and fall as the immune system identifies and deals with threats: the higher the temp, the greater the struggle going on within. In this way, a slight rise in payroll COGS can be seen as an indicator that the company is responding to a stress of some kind—either new competition or a drop in sales, for example. But, like a fever, that spike has to come down quickly. The higher and the more sustained the rise in the COGS percentage, the sicker the company is likely to become.

But you can avoid the illness altogether just by setting up your own COGS-nizance system, and it's not difficult.

Were I to walk into your business today in my role as an executive coach, I'm confident that I could ask very relevant, high-level, and probing financial questions—so long as you provide me with just a few reports, COGS being one of them. With this same report in hand, you too will be able to ask the same questions of yourself, whether you consider yourself to be strong in finance or not. This process for me is called "baselining" your business.

Your income statement keeps you aware of how much money your business makes. I would assume that you have those statements—containing revenue and profit—for each of the last three years. (If you don't, then you haven't been in business that long, and you'll get there.) That's it. That's all the data you need for tracking COGS.

HOW TO CREATE YOUR COGS TABLES

Have your financial department create a spreadsheet for the past three years and the current fiscal year. The input for the spreadsheet will come from your income statement.

The input is total revenue, along with every expense line item's actual numbers for the past three years. Tables 1–3 show a simplified example of the exercise. Table 1 is the actual numbers inputted. Table 2 is the COGS percentage calculation, where each expense item is divided by the revenue in that year to calculate the percentage. Please note that for space reasons I lumped a number of typical expenses under the catch-all of miscellaneous. I *do not* want you to do this. I want you to include *every* expense line, regardless of how big or small it is, and show each one separately. Table 3 includes a target percentage that you will set at the end of the exercise. That's all you need, but you need it all! You need all three tables—not just the actual-numbers table that I'm confident you're seeing already.

TABLE 1: NUMBERS				
	2012	**2013**	**2014**	**2015**
				BUDGET
REVENUE	3,500,000	4,250,000	4,500,000	5,000,000
EXPENSES				
Rent	350,000	350,000	375,000	425,000
Office supplies	14,750	15,000	16,750	17,000
Payroll	1,530,000	2,050,000	2,250,000	2,650,000
Legal	25,000	15,000	40,000	25,000
Accounting	17,500	17,500	18,000	18,000
Depreciation	10,000	10,000	10,000	10,000
Travel	30,000	50,000	50,000	60,000
Meals	3,500	3,400	3,600	4000
Computer	2,500	2,500	2,750	27520
Marketing	10,000	75,000	50,000	100,000
Miscellaneous	500,000	600,000	650,000	675,000
Profit	1,006,750	1,061,600	1,033,900	988,480
Profit %	28.76%	24.98%	22.98%	19.77%

TABLE 2: COGS %				
	2012	**2013**	**2014**	**2015**
Revenue	3,500,000	4,250,000	4,500,000	5,000,000
Expenses				
Rent	10.00%	8.24%	8.33%	8.50%
Office supplies	0.42%	0.35%	0.37%	0.34%
Payroll	43.71%	48.24%	50.00%	53.00%
Legal	0.71%	0.35%	0.89%	0.50%
Accounting	0.50%	0.41%	0.40%	0.36%
Depreciation	0.29%	0.24%	0.22%	0.20%
Travel	0.86%	1.18%	1.11%	1.20%
Meals	0.10%	0.08%	0.08%	0.08%
Computer	0.07%	0.06%	0.06%	0.55%
Marketing	0.29%	1.76%	1.11%	2.00%
Miscellaneous	14.29%	14.12%	14.44%	13.50%
Profit %	28.76%	24.98%	22.98%	19.77%

TABLE 3: TARGET %'s			
	2012	**2013**	**2014**	**2015 Target %**
EXPENSES				
Rent	10.00%	8.24%	8.33%	
Office supplies	0.42%	0.35%	0.37%	
Payroll	43.71%	48.24%	50.00%	
Legal	0.71%	0.35%	0.89%	
Accounting	0.50%	0.41%	0.40%	
Depreciation	0.29%	0.24%	0.22%	
Travel	0.86%	1.18%	1.11%	
Meals	0.10%	0.08%	0.08%	
Computer	0.07%	0.06%	0.06%	
Marketing	0.29%	1.76%	1.11%	
Miscellaneous	14.29%	14.12%	14.44%	
Profit %	28.76%	24.98%	22.98%	

Now that you've looked over the tables, let's review them in detail.

Table 1 is familiar territory, so let's make some high-level observations and one major assumption about it. The assumption: you are managing the business to produce roughly $1 million in profit each year. That's your goal, and you have been consistent at achieving it. Congratulations! One million is a nice number! Here are the observations:

- Revenue is going up—fantastic!

- Employees are being hired and additional leases are being signed—definitely indicators of growth!

- You have committed to increasing your marketing expenses to gain additional leads for your sales department, and all departments will benefit.

- Miscellaneous expenses are growing but not at the expense of profit.

I am going to postulate that a lot of businesses in the entrepreneurial world are run this way, the Table 1 way. It's certainly how I did it for the first 12 years of my entrepreneurial career.

Now, on to Table 2 COGS percentages. This is a different way of looking at fiscal years. It's great Qual Card material for you in your quest to become a *Qualified* Entrepreneur. I am absolutely adamant that you add this disciplined analysis to your repertoire; you won't get me to sign off on your final Entrepreneur Qual Card without it. Comparing percentages is apples to apples and takes out "noise" that comes from fluctuations in revenue. It offers year-over-year comparisons, allowing you to see the trends in how you actually make money. As long as revenue continues to increase in your company year after year, you might be able to get away with never looking at Table 2. But since you are on a self-awareness journey, on your way to becoming a *Qualified* Entrepreneur—and that's someone who makes more disciplined decisions across your organization—let's get into detail.

- The highlighted expense items (Rent and Miscellaneous) are increasing in actual numbers each year, but staying the same or decreasing in percentages, meaning they are not negatively affecting profit percentages.

- Marketing is enjoying a big increase, but is still only 2 percent of your overall expenses. I want you to take note of this because, when times get tight, we often tend to make our first cuts where we have been increasing our spending. That's not a disciplined approach. We need to look at percentages, too. Yes, you are spending almost $100,000 more than you were three years ago, but that's only 1.7 *percent* more. Hunt for bigger game!

- Speaking of percentages, here we go—wow—look at payroll. You have increased your personnel to keep up with growth, and have maintained your $1 million in profit in doing so. But you are now spending 10 percent more in payroll than you were three years ago and your profit has declined by 10 percent in the same period. This is why the COGS percentages are so important. They help you see what's really going on.

By adding the Table 2 COGS percentages report to your monthly review, you'll gain new insight into how your business operates. After becoming familiar with it, you should be able to ask yourself significantly better questions as to how you want to run the business—and you'll ask significantly better questions of your people, too.

Ah, the future. That's Table 3. Now that you've base-lined your business by creating a three-year history of actual numbers and percentages, you get to decide how you want to lead your business moving forward. Here are the guidelines—rules of the road, even—that I offer you:

- The *Qualified* Entrepreneur manages his or her business both by numbers and percentages—always.

- The *Qualified* Entrepreneur manages both actual profit dollars and profit percentage.

I have left the budget percentages blank, as you can see. Go ahead and fill them in. If this were your company, what high-level decision can you make right now, in terms of targeted percentages, looking forward? Would you reduce the payroll percentage or keep it the same? What's your reasoning?

NO MORE HYPOTHETICALS—CREATE YOUR OWN COGS-NIZANCE!

There is a rhythm to most aspects of being a *Qualified* Entrepreneur, and this is most obviously true in areas of financial discipline. Now that you've learned the importance of adding COGS percentages to the actual-numbers trends you're already watching, *do it*. Initiate, if you haven't, a practice of reviewing monthly financial statements that include COGS percentages, and go no further on this journey until you have! Then, at the beginning of each new fiscal year, use the previous year's results to populate a chart like the one below with your up-to-date performance figures. From there it's a snap to update the chart monthly.

	Budget #'s	YTD #'s	Previous Year (#)	2 Years previous (#)	3 Years previous (#)	Current Year Target %	Current Year to Date (%)	Previous Year (%)	2 years Previous (%)	3 Years Previous (%)
Revenue										
Income Statement Categories										
1										
2										
3										
4										
5										
6										
7										
8										
9										
10										

From there it's all a matter of thinking, projecting, and deciding:

- Define the percentage of profit you want to make in your business. You have three years of history and the current year's performance with which to set your goal (if you haven't already).

- Set the target percentage you're willing to spend in each category of expenditure based on your review of past spending and what you are willing to spend this year. Remember, this is a percentage, not a number.

- Analyze. If you are spending too much in one or more categories, you will need to make adjustments to those expenditures or others to ensure that you reach your profit target.

- Revise—make a revised budget. With the total revenue forecasted for the year multiplied by the percentages, you will quickly see what your expenses can reasonably be per category.

These few exercises, detailed in just a few lines and bullets above, saved my first business. I am not exaggerating. They may do the same for yours. All it takes is the willingness and, yes, the discipline, to look at the percentages—not just the numbers—and determine which expenditures are the ones that are driving your business and which are holding it back. COGS-nizance is nothing more than an exercise in seeing the Big Picture. An expense that runs to about .05 percent of your budget is negligible, especially compared to one that exceeds 20 percent. So don't cut where it doesn't matter. And don't invest where it won't help. To get the results you want, you need to spend sensibly. For many of us, especially those of us in services, the make-or-break COGS percentage is that of payroll. Other categories may require as much attention, maybe even more for some of you, but it's my experience and those of my peers that COGS-Payroll is a highly predictive measurement of your company's profit potential. But, however your company's expense percentages shake out, the exercises I've provided you in this chapter are the way to see them clearly, to prioritize them, and to analyze their ups and downs. When it comes time to establish performance targets, you will have at hand all the COGS percentages that will let you use the past to predict the future.

Discipline isn't drudgery, friends. Remember that the way we're defining a *Disciplined* Entrepreneur is . . . *one who commits to becoming ever more self-aware, with the aim of increasing the discipline underlying his or her business decisions.*

CHAPTER 8 QUAL CARD

Initial each requirement as met:

PREREQUISITES INITIALS

The entrepreneur has committed to operating the business with COGS—Cost of Goods Sold—as a focus, fully recognizing that every dollar of COGS savings is equal to one dollar of profit. The entrepreneur understands that the *intent* for defining COGS as all expenses is to get them to understand each of them, rather than to change commonly used terminology in accounting.

_____

The entrepreneur has completed a historical three-year financial COGS chart, including two tables—numbers-only and percentages-only—and the input includes all of the line items from the company income statement and their values.

_____

The entrepreneur is able to fully explain the Table 2 percentage charts, as if going through a "check-out" process. This includes describing in detail the trends in COGS percentages over the past three years, while also establishing and explaining the reasoning behind the budget set-point for the current fiscal year in the Table 3 chart.

_____

The entrepreneur has converted the
budget COGS expense percentage targets
to numbers, based on the fiscal year
revenue goal, and has made necessary
adjustments to come up with the final
approved budget.   _____

Monthly, the entrepreneur is measuring
and reviewing actual-versus-target for the
current fiscal year budget, both numbers
and percentages.   _____

The entrepreneur has placed the three-
year COGS reports into the QE Notebook.   _____

SIGNATURE: _____

DATE: _____

CHAPTER 9

METRICS: MINING FOR GOLD

"The productivity of work is not the responsibility of the worker but of the manager"

—PETER DRUCKER

WHAT ARE THE THREE TO FIVE METRICS BY WHICH YOU RUN YOUR BUSINESS?

I know you've heard this question before; I'm not the first to come up with it or declare the importance of it, but I hope to get you to answer the question with more knowledge and precision than maybe you have before. What I've found in talking with peers and coaching my clients is that many of them struggle to come up with the *right* metrics. Sure, there are some of you, no doubt, who have developed metrics at a very advanced level, choosing ones that are true company-level metrics, ones that reveal plenty about the overall health of your business. But others among you are tracking scads of numbers that give you great detail on *parts* of your business, but tell you almost nothing about the *overall* business.

I well remember being in a hot seat very similar to the one I'm putting you in. Back in my US Navy training days, my captain's question to me was, "What are the most important aspects of the ship you need to monitor to make sure this sub is on its mission and operating well?" The answer varied with circumstances, but the "turnover report" that I provided after a six-hour watch might include:

- The status of the engineering plant, which powers everything aboard the ship.

- Performance results from any training drills we may have conducted during my watch.

- Maintenance tasks and subsequent improvements noted in the performance of a system or device.

- Updates to our navigational plan.

- Anything else that I felt the captain needed to know about how the ship was operating.

Most of the results I expressed in short chronological reports of what happened, and some I reported numerically, with actual measurements, percentages, trend lines, and the like. Or, if the report I gave was subjective—such as saying that the engineering plant was functioning "well," or that we were "on course"—it was almost certainly a judgment I made from looking at actual performance measurements.

I'm sure that metrics aren't a new concept for you. You have heard them referred to as "smart numbers" or "critical numbers," and seen them tracked on the "dashboard" or in a monthly "flash report."

What you call them or how you track them is less important than that you find the *right* metrics.

My first bit of advice to you is not to be afraid to zero in on an unconventional number or ratio. Some of the best metrics are ones that really reveal something important about your individual business. Don't waste time worrying whether your competitors are tracking the same number or ratio. After all, you wouldn't be the first executive to figure out that the metric that "everybody" follows—the one that is supposed to be "common wisdom" in your industry—is wrong for your company.

If you've read the book *Moneyball* or seen the 2011 movie of the same name, you've seen this phenomenon at work.[1] The story shows how data-gathering and new kinds of data have changed the management of professional baseball, led by the Oakland A's, which were once among the poorest franchises in the league— too poor to bid for the biggest names in the game. Yet the A's learned how to compete and become champions by attending to what author Michael Lewis called "the ruthless efficiency that capitalism demands." (I love that phrase.) By use of *sabermetrics*, the team was able to determine which factors really contributed to winning games, and, surprisingly, most of the time-honored stats—stolen bases, runs batted in, and batting averages—weren't at all predictive of baseball stardom. Instead, the A's picked their players on then-obscure factors such as on-base percentage and slugging percentage. In so doing, they paid lower salaries, yet got higher performance on the field.

What the A's did is what we all ought to be doing—casting a skeptical eye on the accepted beliefs of what predicts success in our various industries, and looking carefully at the true drivers in our own companies. What is it, really, that makes your company go? Which metrics tell you at a glance whether things are going well or not so well? For some of you, at least one of the three to five metrics you settle on after researching the possibilities is going to seem unusual, or at least unexpected.

So, let's get down to it. How do you go about identifying the best metrics for your company? Well, the first thing you should know is that nobody can select your metrics for you. Were I sitting with you in your office with data spread out in front of us, I might be able to ask a few helpful questions or point out some interesting ratios just based on my own experience with watching the numbers. But if there's wizardry in this, I surely can't simply lay it out here and show you how to magically arrive at a brilliantly clear picture of your business. No, the only path to good judgment is via knowledge—and knowledge is acquired by spending time, gathering data, and maintaining a long-term focus on the data to ensure that it's useful in managing your business.

> What you may be missing is a productivity metric that helps you achieve that "ruthless efficiency that capitalism demands."

You shouldn't be starting from scratch. From your work in the COGS chapter, you should have at least one or two key measurements that will become part of, or lead you to, your main metrics. In both of my businesses, Payroll COGS was a critical measurement, and my guess is that it will be one of yours, too. No doubt you watch some numbers or ratios from your income statement and balance sheet, as well. What you may be missing, though, is a productivity metric that helps you achieve that "ruthless efficiency that capitalism demands." And we'll get to that.

Growing businesses move through many phases. Contrary to what some entrepreneurs in the go-go early stages believe, there isn't a wrong time for tracking data. Metrics or critical numbers may morph from one category to another depending on where you are in the company life cycle, but it's been my experience that your key or critical numbers will most likely include one of these categories:

- Payroll COGS

- Employee productivity goals

- Income statement targets

- Targets particular to your industry and/or business

And, to be clear, these metrics are company-level metrics, ones that apply to your overall business. Underneath these company-level metrics you should find metrics related to sales, production, marketing, and other functions, departments, or profit centers. You need these too, but they never take the place of company-level metrics.

I have tracked lots of metrics over many years in my two businesses. I could tell you sales figures for each of my offices, with plenty of additional performance information, because I got the figures each month with my income statement, along with other monthly production reports. This data was helpful, but only to a point. Being *lagging* indicators (things that have already happened) they ceased to be useful when the reporting period ended at the end of the business day. They told me nothing about the present or future, and we have only to look at sports—or almost anything else in life—to see that past performance doesn't guarantee current or future success.

Just think for a moment how truly old most of the reporting data you get from your finance department or your accountant is: by the time the month is closed out and the number-crunching has occurred, it could be five days before you see data—and that's not bad at all—or it could be 15, 30, or even 45 days later that the reports hit your desk. Don't get me wrong. Your balance sheet, income statement, and cash-flow statement are crucial reports that you ought to be reviewing monthly. But they are lagging indicators. Along with any metrics you derive from these sources, you must also seek out *leading* indicators. You can't make good financial decisions without having in hand some decent projections of future activity.

> Along with any metrics you derive from these sources, you must also seek out *leading* indicators. You can't make good financial decisions without having in hand some decent projections of future activity.

Take a moment now and fill out the following chart, and do it honestly. What company-level metrics do you currently track, and are they lagging or leading indicators? Also, jot down any targets you may have set in each category.

METRIC	TARGET	LEADING OR LAGGING?

Ideally, the above chart will reflect a mixture of lagging and leading indicators. You should be able to gauge the health of your business looking backward, forward, and straight ahead at today. *If you do not use leading indicators as metrics in your business, you are partially living on hope.* All you can do is cross your fingers that the ship is "steady as she goes." Without data, you've got no factual basis on which to believe that things will continue to go well—none at all.

Let's now zero in on the four types of metrics I identified in the previous bullet points:

Payroll COGS Targets. In Chapter 8, you learned how to develop a COGS report for your business that would reveal the truth as to how your company makes money. You now know, presumably, how many cents on the dollar you spend for each category of expenditure. In this first metric, I want you to define for your business the maximum Payroll COGS you are willing to spend—20 cents, 50 cents, 60 cents, even more? If you have different categories of people, fine; just set a separate metric for each category you have. This is just like establishing a three-year vision for your business.

Just as it's your responsibility to set out a vision for your company, it's yours once again when it comes to setting the target(s) for this metric. (Your financial leader can be a lot of help, though.) When you've done it, you'll have a thorough understanding not just of what your people are costing the business, but what they *ought* to be costing the business in order to meet the profit goal you've already set.

As CEOs, too many of us think only about individual names, titles, and salaries. We need to learn to look at payroll in the aggregate. Only then is it possible to really consider the maximum you're willing to spend from each dollar on employees. As you think about this, don't worry about how you're going to achieve that Payroll COGS metric—that's for later. When the time comes, you can sit down with a trusted financial adviser—someone who knows your business well—or you can hire compensation or incentive experts to assist you in developing a plan. You can even pick the brains of fellow CEOs you meet at Entrepreneurs' Organization, YPO, Vistage, or other leadership organizations. For now, be the *Qualified* Entrepreneur and just set the doggone target. Again, it's very much like the three-year visioning process. You don't need to know at the outset how you're going to get there—you just need to establish where you're going.

> An example: Let's say you set Payroll COGS for your company at 50 percent, meaning you're not going to spend more than 50 cents of every revenue dollar on payroll. (Remember that I'm using percentages and cents-on-the-dollar interchangeably in my financial chapters.) Let me break it down further. You decide to spend 25 percent on compensation for your sales-

people. That means you can spend 25 percent on the rest of the company. Suppose saleswoman Sally is paid $100,000 in salary and brings in $500,000 in revenue. John, meanwhile, is paid $60,000 and brings in $200,000 in revenue. The power of metrics is the ability it gives us to compare apples to apples.

100,000/500,000 = 20 percent. Sally is a relative bargain, because at 20 percent, she is under your 25 percent Payroll COGS target for salespeople. But look at John, who is not as underpaid as he may seem: 60,000/200,000 = 30 percent, exceeding the 25 percent target for Payroll COGS.

Just think: you could create sales incentives for Sally to make more money and, even with the increased pay, she might still not reach 25 cents on the dollar! And this is exactly what you should do—pay your best people more when they are earning it. John's case, however, is the opposite. If he is costing you too much, then at certain revenue levels his base pay or commission level could be cut. These examples reveal the essence of variable pay: the company reduces its fixed costs and increases its variable costs. It's pay-for-performance.

Do not focus on numbers alone—look at the ratios. If circumstances in your business demanded sacrifice, you would make a grave mistake by cutting Sally's pay, and that too often happens when CEOs look only at the raw numbers. Seen from a ratio perspective, she's a productivity winner through and through. If your company isn't making money, she's not the reason; John is. His salary may be low, but the revenue he generates for that pay is even lower. Use ratios in addition to numbers, and you'll be spared the question that keeps you up at night: "Am I paying too much (or too little)?" None of us should want to cut pay just to cut pay. We ought to want our employees to make as much money as they can—so long as it fits the Payroll COGS model we set for our companies.

Employee Productivity Targets (Revenue per Employee, Revenue per Salesperson, Profit per Employee). Employee productivity targets are the ways of judging productivity, and it's the CEO's responsibility to set acceptable levels for the company as a whole. Without them, you're flying blind. To get into this, let me ask you a basic question: Do you want to have more employees paid less, or fewer employees paid more? I know there is no simple answer, but it's an important consideration when you're tackling the issue of productivity. Just as in setting a Payroll COGS target, you can seek advice, but ultimately this is your call. If you want to increase productivity in your business, then you have to put a stake in the ground somewhere and make it a goal, part of your plan. That's first. Then, and only then, can you start to figure out how the target will be achieved. Here is an example of rising sales, accompanied by falling productivity.

TABLE A:

Year	Employees	Revenue	Revenue/ Employee	Sales-people	Revenue/ Salesperson	Profit	Profit/ Employee
1	75	$7.5 million	$100,000	30	$250,000	$750,000	$10,000
2	100	$8.5 million	$85,000	40	$212,500	$800,000	$8,000
3	125	$9.5 million	$76,000	50	$190,000	$850,000	$6,800

TABLE B:

Year	Employees	Revenue	Revenue/ Employee	Sales-people	Revenue/ Salesperson	Profit	Profit/ Employee
1	75	$7.5 million	$100,000	30	$250,000	$750,000	$10,000
2	100	$8.5 million	$85,000	40	$212,500	$800,000	$8,000
3	125	$9.5 million	$76,000	50	$190,000	$850,000	$6,800
4	125	$11.25 million	$90,000	50	$225,000	$950,000	$7,600
5	125	$12.5 million	$100,000	50	$250,000	$1,100,000	$8,800

What is your first reaction to the numbers in Table A the previous page? Do you notice, with approval, the sales and profit growth? How long does it take you to notice the falling productivity? Lastly, do these productivity numbers look uncomfortably familiar? We entrepreneurs love growth in any form, so many of us will pay special attention to the sales figures. But, to become a *Qualified* Entrepreneur who functions well as the CEO of an organization that is both growing and maturing, we need to shift to more of a focus on individual efficiency and overall productivity. It's crucial, as Table A shows. Here, growth has driven the workforce to demand more hiring, and leading an ever-larger organization feels like success to the entrepreneur-turned-CEO. But, stop and think: What do you want your company to look like? Big is good, but big and efficient is much, much better. I've added Years 4 and 5 to Table B, which shows how a determined CEO can reverse the slide in productivity.

I hope this example inspires you to *mine your data*—to find out what you've really accomplished over the last several years of growth. However profitable your company may be, you will likely see room for improvement. And now that you have set COGS goals, it's almost a certainty that the gap between the goal and the status quo will be significant. So, find out which numbers and ratios are the most telling for your line of business, plug them into a spreadsheet for as many years as you have the data, and set goals. Start today using what you've got and make adjustments and improvements as time goes on. *Remember, numbers tell you what you've accomplished. Ratios tell you how efficiently you have accomplished your numbers.* Both are important.[2, 3]

Income Statement Numbers (Lagging Indicators). I have to assume that you are much more familiar with these than other metrics, and that you have gotten into a routine of measuring and tracking revenue, profit, gross margin, operating expenses, and so on. All of this is great data, so long as you continually remind yourself that these are snapshots of the past. I would like you to have a plan built on at least three years of income statement data—for that is how budgets ought to be made! It's sad but true: managers and department heads often ascribe to the "budget it or lose it" mantra. So, instead of beginning your budget cycle by letting people declare what they intend to spend, use your data! Complete the chart below using your company's historical performance.

Income Statement Category	Historical COGS %	Target COGS %	Current Year Expense Target (Budget)	Fiscal Year-to-Date Expenses	Fiscal Year-to-Date COGS (%)	Variance (%)

I'll say it again: any data is gold. Three years of data is platinum— rare earth! Numbers don't lie, they tell a story—especially when you have enough history in front of you to show trends.

When check-out time arrives and your "captain" asks you which metrics are the ones by which you run your business, it's not enough to have three to five numbers or ratios to cite. You have to be able to explain *why* these are the right numbers.

> Numbers don't lie, they tell a story—especially when you have enough history in front of you to show trends.

Before leaving this chapter, let's touch on some external data that you should be watching to help inform the decisions you make internally:

- **Economic data.** This includes both federal and state unemployment rates and gross domestic product (GDP), as well as any report that would have a direct impact on your particular business. Such external data helps you spot changes in the business cycle that affect your company. Often, changes in national numbers can foretell market shifts in local markets and within industries.

- **Industry data.** Most industries track their own set of indicators, and you should become expert in mining them for the planning data they can provide. For example, in the semiconductor industry there is a book-to-bill index. If it is greater than 1, then orders have exceeded production and the industry is expanding. If it is less than 1, then production is exceeding orders and there is now or soon will be an oversupply condition that foretells an industry slowdown. Watch not only numbers but trends, because that's how you can anticipate which way the industry is going—up or down.

- **Market Data.** What percentage of the market is yours? Is your market growing or contracting, and what is the three-year projection for overall market revenue and share for the top companies in your market? Are you dominant, are you gaining ground, or are you losing share to the competition? Is there room for growth? Or have you maxed out in a dying industry? There's money to be made in any situation—so long as you know which one you're in!

As I bring this chapter to a close—and with it, the Financial Leadership section of the book—I can almost hear the distant cheering. I know you're out there, you numbers-averse entrepreneurs! And I hope that I've been able to show you that tracking numbers, analyzing them, and using them to both set goals and evaluate your company's progress toward achieving them is easier than you have previously believed. Moreover, I hope I've convinced you that establishing a financial discipline in your company doesn't make your job more complicated or take you away from the sales and marketing that is probably your first and longest-lasting love. On the contrary, financial discipline shows you where to go and how to get there.

CHAPTER 9 QUAL CARD

Initial each requirement as met:

PREREQUISITES   INITIALS

The entrepreneur has compiled a list of all
metrics currently used or monitored in the
business in a spreadsheet, adding a column
for naming the person accountable for
setting baseline data for each metric.   _____

The entrepreneur has compiled a
(minimum) three-year report on the
metrics in his/her business pertaining to
Payroll COGS and Employee Productivity (both at the company and salesperson
levels) and set targets for the current fiscal
year. The entrepreneur is using these two
reports as a training ground, embracing
the trend analysis and decision making
that occurs while completing this exercise,
and adding additional customized metrics
to the three-year metric report.   _____

The entrepreneur has added the three-
year metric and Payroll COGS report to the
QE Notebook.   _____

The entrepreneur has established a minimum of three and as many as five company-level leading indicator metrics that are specific to his/her business.   _____

The entrepreneur has researched and determined market data for his/her business's industry, to include overall market size, three-year projections to track trends, and market-share data for top competitors.   _____

SIGNATURE: _____

DATE: _____

CHAPTER 10

VALUES-BASED LEADERSHIP

"Your beliefs become your thoughts. Your thoughts become your words. Your words become your actions. Your actions become your habits. Your habits become your values. Your values become your destiny."

—MAHATMA S. GANDHI

Why, you might ask, is a chapter about values stuck here, in the latter part of the book? Shouldn't it be right up front? Aren't core values something you handle in the early months of a new company?

Well, yes and no. There are a couple of reasons why you find the topic here.

First, I'm assuming that if you're involved enough in running a business that you'd take time to read this book, you're not lacking for a set of "core values"—namely, 3–10 statements that define your business and guide how you and your employees conduct it.[1] I doubt that I need to teach you the subject or sell you on the concept. You probably have your company's values listed and framed somewhere in the office. Maybe they're on the back of your company's business cards, too. And if you're really living your core values as the leader of the enterprise, your organization is filled with people who share those values with you.

But second, and more to the point, core values are *not* just an early-phase thing. I put this chapter here because your core values should be alive and a part of all that you and your company do. They should be a constant presence from startup to corporate maturity. Taken collectively, they should form the strong linchpin that holds your organization together. Yet at the same time, your core values should seem perpetually current and relevant—no matter where you are in your business cycle or what your present circumstances may be. And that's the hard part—remembering to periodically hit "refresh" and experience your core values, with meaning, today and every day.

ARE YOUR CORE VALUES RELEVANT?

Stop and consider whether your core values are withstanding the test of time. Have your company's values stayed valid and relevant? Or have you allowed them to retreat a bit each year, to the point that they're out of sight and out of mind? Can your people still recite your list of core values? Heck, can *you*? Do you and your company actively live them?

You'll notice that I didn't ask whether your core values had become irrelevant. I'm not sure that's even possible. The core values you established early in the life of your company are, like our own personal values and traits, fairly immutable. Where values are concerned, we don't wake up some morning and say, "Actually, I don't think I believe in respect anymore"—or integrity, or fair play, or whatever. What happens, instead, is that core values are relegated to a frame on the wall and not much talked about. Then, in the course of business, things happen to whittle away at the spirit and sense of what your company stands for.

Anybody who has been in business for more than a few years knows what I'm talking about. Like me, you have probably experienced the internal and external pressures that can put a set of core values to the test. Harry M. Jansen Kraemer Jr., a noted commentator on values-based leadership, the former CEO of Baxter International, and a current professor at Northwestern University's Kellogg School of Management, speaks of the three Cs—change, controversy, and crisis—and their propensity to degrade core values or cause them to be left behind. He says it takes a fourth C, courage, to keep values at the forefront of your managerial task. So ask yourself here and now: Do you and your company still live by your core values, or have you compromised and cut corners to the point that the words have become fairly meaningless?[2, 3, 4]

Author Jim Collins has this test for whether a value can be considered core: Would you want to hold these core values, even if at some point one or more of them became a competitive disadvantage, and you will take a financial hit in your business to live your core values?[5]

Ideally, each of us should be able to stand firm on our core values, despite changes in products or services, strategy, or personnel. Your industry may pivot and the economy may shift, but your values should stay put. And I'll take a stand right here and agree with what has been written about core values for years: anybody who knowingly violates your company's core values, at any time or for any reason, should be at risk of being fired for that violation. That goes for you as founder or CEO, too. You can and probably should be removed from your position for any significant infraction of the values you inherited or helped put in place.

Since Jim Collins introduced the concept of core values in his 1994 landmark book *Built to Last*, companies have made the establishment of core values a routine exercise, usually paired with the development of a mission statement. In the business press, core values associated with large or influential companies have taken on a life of their own, especially when colorfully expressed. Zappos, the online shoe and apparel retailer, is famous for its desire to "deliver WOW" and "create . . . a little weirdness."[6] Apple drives grammar-conscious observers crazy with its "Think Different" value/slogan.[7] Companies such as Patagonia and Ben and Jerry's have elevated core values pertaining to environmental stewardship almost to the level of a brand.[8, 9] And I think many of us have enjoyed a chuckle in recent years when considering Google's formal corporate motto of "Don't be evil."[10]

Entrepreneurs, being the visionaries and creators that we are, are great at establishing core values—if you get us to slow down long enough to put some thought into it! But my guess is that most of us created our core values with only positive outcomes in mind. In the excitement of a new enterprise, and amid the exuberance of early success, it's difficult to envision the business struggling through the three Cs or being tempted by situations that would compromise core values. Unlike the news on TV, where the focus tends to be on the negative, in an entrepreneur's world everything's comin' up roses. There's no "can't do" or "won't succeed." It's just not how we roll. How could we get a company off the ground if we weren't relentlessly confident and positive?

But, as I've already indicated, there is a dark side to entrepreneurship. There are times when things get truly rough, times when real disciplined leadership is required to stay on the straight and narrow. And I know that if you haven't experienced darker days yet, you likely will. Forewarned is forearmed: I think it's to every leader's advantage to anticipate the challenges and give some early thought as to how they will be met. Will your core values continue to live and breathe, or will they be relegated to gathering dust in a frame? Consider the pithy paragraph I found at the bottom of a yourdictionary.com definition of core values: "While some people or companies might expressly publish their core values, often the best way to identify these values is by how they act and behave. *A core value is only a true core value if it has an active influence and if the people or company manage to live by it, at least most of the time.*"

Here's an example of a company living its core values, one I was lucky to see in the news during the writing of this chapter. (Since integrity is one of my core values, you know I'm not fibbing about the timing!) CVS, the drugstore chain, announced that its stores would stop selling cigarettes.[11] Why? They are continuing to metamorphose into a retail-based health-care provider, offering more minute clinics and wellness advice to customers. To stay true to the core values associated with their new mission of becoming a top tier provider in the health and wellness industry, they are willingly sacrificing a projected $2 billion in smoking-related revenues during the first fiscal year of the policy shift. Two billion!

Ask yourself: How much revenue would *you* sacrifice to uphold the core values of your business?

There are many ways to see your core values tested. Certainly it happens when one of your salespeople brings you an opportunity that is clearly in the gray zone—something that would make you money, but at the same time would compromise everything that you and your company stand for. That's a time when you really have to stop and think about whether you're going to take the step. But it also happens subtly, when you're just not looking, when growth is so strong and so fast that you don't recognize that you've gradually crossed the line…until the day comes when you can barely find your way back.

Want to avoid that? Well, then, take the ancient Greek saying "know thyself" to heart.

HOW WELL DO YOUR COMPANY'S VALUES MATCH YOUR OWN?

The best way to hold the line on your company's core values in the face of temptation and change is to have selected values that are congruent with your personal credo. I believe this, and so do others who have addressed the subject, including Northwestern University's Harry Kraemer. Says he, in one of his opinion pieces for *Forbes*, " . . . becoming the best kind of leader isn't about emulating a role model or a historic figure.[12, 13, 14] Rather, your leadership must be rooted in who you are and what matters most to you. When you truly know yourself and what you stand for, it is much easier to know what to do in any situation. It always comes down to doing the right thing and doing the best you can."

So stop and think: As the leader of your organization, what principles guide you? I'm sure most of us come up with things like achieving excellence or making a contribution to society. We may think about the ways we'd like our companies to help others achieve their goals or of operating the business under the rules of fair play. Those are all positive motivators. But it pays to think now and then about the things that motivate us that are ego-driven and not completely positive. Are you motivated by pride of performance, or by winning a competitive battle? Is it building a legacy that spurs you on? Or is it something as simple as money or fame that drives you?

The best way to hold the line on your company's core values in the face of temptation and change is to have selected values that are congruent with your personal credo.

These are all good things to know about yourself as founder or CEO. That's because your company will likely display some of the same tendencies you do. Is that good or bad? The only way to judge is by thinking through your own traits in relation to the core values you have established—or would want to establish—for your company.

The past decade and a half has brought us plenty of very public examples of companies that have lost their way, ethically speaking:[15, 16, 17]

- Directors and executives of Enron, the 1990s energy giant, fraudulently concealed large financial losses, landing some of its leaders in prison after charges came to light in 2001.

- Accounting firm Arthur Andersen was convicted of obstructing justice for shredding documents in 2002 to try to protect its major client Enron.

- Several hedge fund company founders and managers were convicted of insider trading in 2012 and 2013.

- Halliburton and subsidiary KBR, a defense contractor, was found guilty of bribery and over-charging the government in no-bid contracts, all stemming from the Iraq war that began in 2003.

- In 2006, HP's CEO ordered board members spied upon to determine the source of leaks.

- Former Tyco International CEO Leo Kozlowski— known for a $2 million birthday party mostly paid for by his company—was convicted in 2005 of crimes related to receiving $81 million in unauthorized bonuses, the purchase of art for over $14 million, and the payment by Tyco of a $20 million investment banking fee to a former Tyco director. He served more than six years in prison.

- Bernard Ebbers, the founder of telecommunications giant Worldcom, was convicted in 2005 of fraud, conspiracy, and filing false documents with regulators— all related to an $11 billion accounting scandal.

- Investor and fund owner Bernie Madoff is serving a 150-year sentence for operating a Ponzi scheme that is estimated to have cost his investors $18 billion.

- The military isn't exempt from ethical problems, either. During the writing of this book, Air Force nuclear officers acknowledged widespread cheating on competency exams, and Army recruiting officers were accused of receiving kickbacks.

Bear in mind that this list is aimed at illustrating major violations of what had to be the core values of these organizations, and usually, the law. It's a list that would have grown much longer had I included more CEO misdeeds leading to scandal—or the numerous fraud and malfeasance allegations stemming from the most recent financial crisis.

What happened in these companies? A number of things, I'm sure. Market pressures perhaps caused people up and down the chain of command to lose sight of their core values or to make a conscious judgment that "breaking the rules" wouldn't last long and would serve the greater good of preserving or growing the company. But I'd also submit that these CEOs and others did too good a job of separating the company's values from their own.

Let's think about that for a moment. In many circumstances we would consider it a good thing, a sign of managerial maturity, when an entrepreneur learns to run the company as less of an extension of himself or herself. In fact, I've made that part of the description of a *Qualified* Entrepreneur. But it seems to me that **ethics and values are very good places, healthy places, for a founder or CEO to maintain a shared identity with the company.**

Here are some of my personal core values, which have been the core values of my companies as well:

- **Work hard first, then play.** Delayed gratification is a discipline that yields great results. There are no shortcuts to success.

- **Never make the same mistake twice.** Learning from past mistakes is critical. I have plenty of mistakes left in me, just hopefully not the ones I have made in the past!

- **The Golden Rule.** Treat people as you want to be treated yourself.

- **Respect must be earned.** For me, this concept dates back to my navy days, and it's as true for me as CEO as it is for any of my employees.

- **Humility, not arrogance.** I strongly believe (and I taught my children this) that nobody is better than anybody else. Everybody in an organization is important and has a role to play. To succeed, I need to take more risk and work harder and smarter and more consistently over a long period of time.

- **Honesty and integrity first, last, and always.** My office has long featured a framed quote that gives one of these words real utility for me:

  "Integrity is one of several paths. It distinguishes itself from others because it is the right path, and the only one upon which you will never get lost." —M. H. McKee

- **Enduring principles.** I find meaning for this value in a former president's advice, also long a feature in my office:

"In matters of style, swim with the currents . . . in matters of principle, stand like a rock." —Thomas Jefferson

- **Try your best, always.** I think Northwestern's Harry Kraemer says it well:[18, 19, 20]

  "By knowing myself and my values, being committed to balance and having true self-confidence and genuine humility, I can far more easily make decisions, no matter if I'm facing a crisis or an opportunity. The answer is always simply to do the right thing and the very best that I can."

  And here's one more that I find inspiring:

  "We are what we repeatedly do. Excellence, then, is not an act, but a habit." —Attributed to Aristotle

As we leave this chapter, I invite you to ask yourself which core values guide you when it's crunch time on a major decision. If you're not sure, if the words don't quickly come to mind, it might be time to dust off your core values, get reacquainted with them, and evaluate whether they are vital and vibrant enough to take you into the next phase of your company's life. Someday you will face a choice of the type I've described in this chapter. Someday you will find out—if you haven't already—how far you'll go to defend your personal and corporate core values and whether or not you're willing to risk revenue growth, market value, and increased profit to do it.

Never forget the old adage that a *Qualified* Entrepreneur knows well: **it takes a lifetime to build a reputation, and a minute to lose it.**

CHAPTER 10 QUAL CARD

Initial requirements as met:

PREREQUISITES   INITIALS

The entrepreneur has conducted an audit
of his/her company's core values to ensure
they are actively influential in company
policies and that the people of the organization live by them.   _____

The entrepreneur has developed his/her
own personal value statements.   _____

The entrepreneur has established consistent and company-wide training on the
business's core values and has communicated to employees that decisions to hire,
fire, train, and promote will be based on
adherence to these core values.   _____

The entrepreneur has made a list of past
decisions that have been consistent with
maintaining core values and have caused a
direct financial hit on the business.   _____

The entrepreneur has made a list of the kinds of decisions he/she may need to make, noting potential conflict between the company's revenue growth and its core values. From this a list of possible actions and responses has been developed, that is, "If this happens, I would do this."

SIGNATURE: _____

DATE: _____

CHAPTER 11

CAREER-LONG LEARNING

"Smart men learn from their mistakes,
wise men learn from others'."

—JIM BUCK, FORMER ARMY OFFICER,
FELLOW ENTREPRENEURS' ORGANIZATION
PARTICIPANT, AND FRIEND.

How did you like school when you were growing up? Did you get good grades? Would you say that you lived up to your potential? Or was school something you just put up with and got through? While the latest statistics show that a majority of entrepreneurs have at least a bachelor's degree, there are plenty of reports out there to suggest that some entrepreneurs were only average students, and some of the most notable among us couldn't wait to get out of school and on with life. Names like, oh, Gates, Jobs, Dell . . . entrepreneurs who are also some of the business world's best-known college dropouts.

Would you be surprised to see the dropout Bill Gates advocating for a form of career-long learning? He does, as you will see.

In my own life, I've recognized deficits in both kinds of learning—the formal and the experiential. When I first became qualified to drive a submarine, I'd had 15 months of training but absolutely zero hands-on experience. I knew what to do but I'd never done it, so I started out as a trainee, standing watch "Under Instruction," so that my every move could be overseen by higher-rank officers who knew the ropes. Then, when I became an entrepreneur, it was the opposite—I had precisely zilch advanced business training from 1991 to 1998, but I had tactical experience coming out of my ears. *I didn't think I needed anybody's help*—until I started facing difficult decisions and, at times, making mistakes.

> *I didn't think I needed anybody's help—until I started facing difficult decisions and, at times, making mistakes.*

Ah, mistakes and submarines in the same paragraph—it reminds me of a story from my navy days.

As you might imagine, going to the bathroom on a sub isn't just a matter of going and then flushing, as you would at home. When we "flush the toilet" on a submarine, we pull back a handle not unlike the one-armed bandits in a casino full of slot machines. This motion opens a ball valve. If you're not familiar with ball valves, picture a ball with openings at each side. When the valve is closed, the ball is solid and nothing passes through it. When the handle pulls back, the holes align, and you can see straight through it. In that position, the toilet's contents pour into the ship's sanitary tanks. Eventually the tanks become full, of course, requiring that they be emptied at sea via air at high pressure. During such times, we hang a sign on the bathroom that says "Blowing sanitary." Think about why:

if somebody pulls back that handle and opens the valve during the clean-out . . . well, what's in the tanks will end up in the bathroom, and with considerable force. Not a pretty picture.

One night I was lying in my rack (that's my bed, civilians) when I heard a terrible racket. Yep, somebody was working on some maintenance in our bathroom and forgot the "blowing sanitary" sign they'd passed on the way in. That somebody now had the contents of Sanitary Tank 1 all over themselves and the bathroom. Uh, it was "Clean-up, Aisle 5!" (After that, I reflexively leaned waaaayyy back every time I pulled that handle, just in case.)

I remember thinking, "Wow, he'll never make that mistake again." But he did. Some time later it happened again, and oh how his immediate superior berated him! I felt really badly for the guy at the time, but it wasn't long into my career as an officer before I began feeling he actually deserved much more than he'd gotten. We all make mistakes, we learn from them, and move on. To continue to make the same mistake . . . ? It's flat-out unacceptable, because it represents an inability or unwillingness to learn.

Moral of the story: don't be that guy. We all need to try not to be that guy.

So, what mistakes are you making as the entrepreneurial CEO of your organization? Are you learning from your mistakes, or, like some sort of real-world *Groundhog Day* movie, do you feel doomed to repeat them again and again? More importantly, do you feel you're taking the right steps to avoid making mistakes in the first place?

I bless the day I decided to sign up for the Entrepreneurs' Organization's Birthing of Giants (BOG) program. I did it out of curiosity, really, hoping mostly to meet and spend time with folks who love starting companies as much as I do. It was incredible for that. But, as I've already told you earlier in the book, BOG was a huge wake-up-and-smell-the-coffee moment for me. I had my mind blown by all that I was doing wrong or simply not doing. It really shook my confidence—but in a good way.

> **Truth to tell, one of my goals with this book is to similarly pull you out of your comfort zone, to give each of you your own personalized BOG experience.**

Truth to tell, one of my goals with this book is to similarly pull you out of your comfort zone, to give each of you your own personalized BOG experience. My goal has been to get you thinking about whether you are truly prepared to run your organization as it grows and changes—assuming that you do want to run it, of course. In 1999, when my ego barely survived the first week of BOG, I had to face the fact that I was not fully prepared for the job. And remember: my company Orion International was wildly successful at that point. Any mistakes I was making weren't obvious—until the coursework began pointing them out to me.

My Second Decision was made at the end of that first BOG gathering. I had to admit to myself that there was much "I didn't know what I didn't know" (IDKWIDK). I had to commit to a much more disciplined approach to the management and leadership of Orion. And in doing this, I went all-in on becoming a

Qualified Entrepreneur and have never looked back. Regardless of your true feelings for or against "school," my hope is that you too will make the Second Decision with the help of this book.

More than 15 years have passed since that scary first week of BOG—that's 15-plus years of OJT (on-the-job training), augmented by plenty of classroom instruction and mentorship. As my career progressed, I learned that as a wannabe Steady/Proactive leader, I had to seek out the advice and experience of others who had gone before me in this role—and I wanted to! I became a sponge. I became determined to learn all that I could to avoid or at least minimize the classic mistakes made by entrepreneurs in growing their own businesses.

Now, I suspect there are some of you for whom the very mention of "mistakes" gets your back up. Maybe you don't quite accept that you make mistakes. Maybe you prefer synonyms like "course corrections" or "false starts." Maybe you also prefer the pronoun "we" to "I" when talking about, *er*, errors. If I'm talking about you here, I have another set of questions for your consideration:

- As president/CEO/owner/founder, do you think you have to be all-knowing? Should you have all the answers, all the time?

- If a situation stumps you, does it make you feel weak or inadequate?

- Do you take offense if somebody questions you or challenges your point of view?

- Does it make you uncomfortable to have people around you who may be smarter than you?

We all know the right answer to these questions; it's "no" straight down the line. But I'm asking you to think about the answers that are real and true . . . for you. If there are some yeses, you need to begin your education process by cutting yourself some slack. Nobody executes flawlessly, and the few who get close usually have help.

Think about this from the perspective of parenting for a minute. Whether you're a parent yourself or not, you know that it's a role riddled with the potential for making mistakes. Worse, many of those mistakes are ones that you absolutely can't make twice, lest you risk the kid's life or future. In parenting, not learning is not an option. And what do you expect of your kids? Do you teach them to avoid the mistakes you've made? Do you try to prevent them from making the same mistake twice? I'm sure the answers are "yes" and "of course!" And how do you respond if the kid gives you an attitude, as if they already know everything? Well, I can only speak for myself. Sometimes I made the unpopular decision of "my way or the highway"—but that's why parents get the big bucks, right? More often, seeing the ridiculousness of teenaged stubbornness, it was, "Heh, good luck with that!"

That's sort of how I come down when a corporate leader acts as though continuing education for entrepreneurs isn't necessary or even desirable: "What?! Well, hey, go for it!"

Here's how I see the situation: in the corporate world of today with its many complexities, it's school or "be schooled." If you are not attending classes, learning from your peers, and studying to master the craft of being a *Qualified* Entrepreneur, then watch out, because those around you *are*, and they will soon surpass you in all the ways that matter. Athletes work on form, physiology, and kinesthetic knowledge their entire careers. Surgeons devote time each year to continuing education. So should you!

Any professional works continually to improve. Each of us has to work to "up our game," because standing still means falling behind. Education isn't easy for entrepreneurs like us, not least because it means we'll hear things we don't want to hear about our methods and strategies. But the willingness to put one's self in that kind of exposed, vulnerable position is what separates mere entrepreneurs from *Qualified* Entrepreneurs. Remember, the first step toward becoming a *Qualified* Entrepreneur is your graduation to *Disciplined* Entrepreneur. The disciplined ones work within a structure that is built of integrity, harnessed ambition, and yes, tested knowledge—the kind that comes from a commitment to lifelong learning.

> *"There are two kinds of success; one is the very rare kind that comes to the person who has the power to do what no one else has - the power to do that is genius. But the average person who wins what we call success is not a genius. That person is a man or woman who has merely the ordinary qualities that they share with their fellows, but who has developed these ordinary qualities to more than ordinary degree."*
>
> —THEODORE ROOSEVELT

YOUR ENTREPRENEURIAL EDUCATION TIMELINE/LIFELINE

Remember our concept of a "lifeline," which is actually a timeline pertaining to some aspect of your life or career. Previously we looked at your Career/Professional Lifeline. Now I want to share with you my Entrepreneurial Education Lifeline, and invite you to create your own.

ENTREPRENEURIAL EDUCATION TIMELINE/LIFELINE

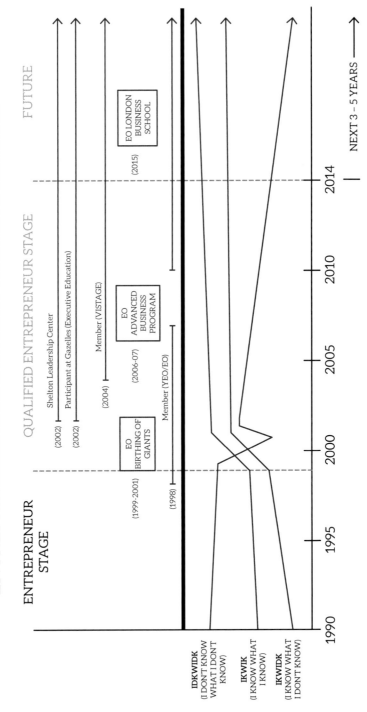

ENTREPRENEURAL EDUCATION TIMELINE/LIFELINE

NEXT 3 – 5 YEARS ⟶

My timeline depicts, through various types of learning experience, my efforts to become a *Qualified* Entrepreneur. It starts with on-the-job training (OJT), which helped me distinguish between "I don't know what I don't know" (IDKWIDK), "I know what I know" (IKWIK), and "I know what I don't know" (IKWIDK).

My zeal for education and personal development is obvious here. In addition to BOG, I am a founding member of the Raleigh-Durham chapter of Entrepreneurs' Organization, and in 2004 I joined Vistage. I have always been a huge supporter of Gazelles, Inc., led by Verne Harnish, and have been a member of the Board of Advisors of the General H. Hugh Shelton Leadership Center at NC State since 2002, surrounding myself with great leaders from whom I am continually learning, and with whom I share the passion for Values Based Leadership that the Shelton Center is built upon.[1] I simply cannot overstate the value of these organizations in helping me to succeed as an entrepreneur, develop my leadership skills, and assist others in doing the same.

Once again, I have left a blank page for you to add your own education timeline. Don't worry if there's not much to put on it. This book can be your start! I also invite you to try using transparencies or tracing paper to overlay and combine your Entrepreneurial Education Lifeline with your Career/Professional Lifeline. As you did with your career timeline, extend the education timeline out three to five years. The comparison can lead to observations, and here are mine:

- My starter years as an entrepreneur consisted of consistent hyper-growth even as I was at the peak of my "I don't know what I don't know" (IDKWIDK) period.

- Since 1998, with my involvement with the Entrepreneurs' Organization and Vistage, I have spent thousands of hours with other CEOs, working alongside them and sharing our common issues and concerns. This provided me focused and dedicated CEO "think time" during profitable and unprofitable times, and through both down and up cycles in the economy. Even as I've improved my own personal capacity as a leader, I've assisted in the development of others' capacities— and all of our organizations have benefited from the improved versions of us, their CEOs.

- I have had a personal coach through Vistage for more than 10 years as of this writing.

- Over 15-plus years and as the result of my involvement in CEO peer groups across every phase of business startup and growth, I have transitioned from an ultra-confident and potentially arrogant young entrepreneur to a *Qualified* Entrepreneur—with all that implies. For me, one of the most important outcomes of this educational journey is learning to surround myself with people who will tell me what I *need* to hear instead of what they think I *want* to hear.

- My career-long learning continues...forever. You can see that I am attending the EO London Business School in 2015 with 70 other global entrepreneurs... my learning continues even after building and selling two companies...that is what career-long learning truly means!

Let's divide the points of view on entrepreneurial education by the types of entrepreneur:

Urgent/Reactive: This leader can't even consider getting some schooling—there's too much to do, too many fires to put out. Maybe sometime in the future, when things become less hectic (which is never, given this personality type).

Ever Optimistic: This person already has it figured out and, therefore, struggles to see the value in education or training. Things can't possibly be better! He or she is already kicking butt and taking names in business, so why mess with success? But there's another form of this personality type, too. This one might thoroughly enjoy affiliating with a group of entrepreneurs because they get to hang out with peers who can push them to even higher accomplishments, because he or she is "so successful" and has "so much to offer," or simply because it's fun and ego-boosting to say "I'm part of the group." (When I joined the Entrepreneur's Organization this was my personality type, and some of it still lives with me today!)

> Steady/Proactive knows that we learn from both good things and bad, and he or she sees the inherent value of learning navigation, so to speak, from someone who has managed to cross the proverbial sea.

Reflexively Pessimistic: This type, being a natural worrier, has a painfully realistic view of the business and can see every wart or deficiency in his or her leadership. Courses on risk management and operational efficiency are the sorts of things that draw this leader, but really, this type is more open than most to learning on any topic, and is also open to receiving some of that learning from peers and others. Fear is a great motivator!

Steady/Proactive: Then there's the optimal type of leader who says, "Bring it on, teach me! Let me learn best practices from the best and how to avoid mistakes from those who have already made them!" Steady/Proactive knows that we learn from both good things and bad, and he or she sees the inherent value of learning navigation, so to speak, from someone who has managed to cross the proverbial sea.

I would venture to say that each type of leader, deep down, wants to learn from others. But there's always something in the way, whether it's time or a perceived lack of need or value in whatever educational opportunity is being presented. And reality paints another aspect into the picture: People just don't want to ask for help. Too many of us view entrepreneurial education as a cry for help—and those who partake of it somehow weak or ready to admit defeat.

All of which brings me to two more questions for you to consider in your quiet moments:

- If you concede that you don't know everything, can you wrap your head around the idea that it actually might be a sign of strength to admit it?

- Who challenges you? Do you have peers, mentors, or advisers who play that role? Or are you going it alone?

As I pose these questions, I'm really hoping that you've already experienced some significant setback or failure in your career. Only then is it really possible, I think, to see yourself as vulnerable to circumstances—be they out there in the market, or "in" there, stemming from your own deficiencies as a leader. Only when you have failed to some degree do you know whether you can pick yourself up and move on and, more importantly, whether you're going to do that on your own or with the help of others. Some of us just won't seek help from others until we're truly feeling human, fallible . . . vulnerable.

NEVER, EVER MAKE THE SAME MISTAKE TWICE

This book wouldn't exist without my own failures—the lessons I've learned from them, the value I've found in accepting my vulnerability, and, most of all, my determination that no mistake should ever be repeated, by me, the guy in the submarine's bathroom, or anyone else! Lifelong learning is my goal, and my credo is, "Never make the same mistake twice."

"The measure of success is not whether you have a tough problem to deal with, but whether it's the same problem you had last year." — John Foster Dulles

We're all familiar with the old definition of insanity: doing the same things over and over and expecting different results. Right? Yet, that's a type of insanity that is very familiar to many of us as entrepreneurs and peer-group participants! By far the most frustrating episodes I've experienced in peer groups are those where the CEO keeps bringing us the same issue, year after year. It's rare, but it happens. What's even more frustrating is the fact that most of these CEOs end up angry and choose to leave the group. Everyone in the room—except the CEO—can see that the company is stagnant and perennially falling short of its potential, and everybody—except the CEO—knows that the problem is at the top.

So, my challenge to you is to look at the following list and find your current attitude toward entrepreneurial education or your current level of involvement with it, and consider what else on the list may work for you. I've coded all but the first two (which aren't education) into three categories: Accountability (A), Consultation (C), and Teaching (T). Yes, the abbreviations spell out "ACT"—which is exactly what I would want you as *a Qualified* Entrepreneur to do!

- **No school, ever.** "This is my business, and I will build it and run it exactly as I want, with no outside influence." Needless to say, I've got a problem with this one.

- **OJT.** "I learn as I go." If OJT really is your only learning strategy, you are dooming your company to fall short of its potential, pure and simple.

- **The Amazon degree program.** (T) "I read a lot on leadership subjects." Well, I'm surely not going to criticize book buyers (for obvious reasons), and I'm an avid business book reader myself. But I have to ask: Is your bookshelf a "working bookshelf," or just a showcase?

- **Conferences/seminars.** (T) There are plenty of these on various topics, scheduled at times and locations convenient to most. The benefits range from skill building to networking, from informational to motivational. You choose what adds value to your career and your organization.

- **Informal consultants and advisers.** (A/C) "I have a couple of people I trust." You may not always appreciate it when they disagree with you, but it at least helps to have somebody to talk to.

- **CEO peer groups.** (A/T/C) Roundtable groups such as EO, Vistage, Young Presidents' Organization, and chambers of commerce allow you to join fellow entrepreneurs/presidents/CEOs in a confidential setting to learn from one another. You remain in complete control of your destiny, and your level of accountability to the group varies with the expectations of the organization.

- **Coaching.** (A) In a TED talk, Microsoft founder (and college dropout) Bill Gates voiced his belief that every leader needs a one-on-one relationship with someone who can help move your business forward—and hold you accountable when you back off of promised action. The coaching can be long or short term, goal oriented or aimed at providing general support, and a place to vent. But one of the richest men in the world swears by it, which ought to make it worth trying.

- **Mentors.** (C/T) Unlike coaches who are paid, mentors usually provide guidance from their own experience while asking nothing in return (except perhaps friendship). If you're lucky enough to get taken under the wing of a good mentor, find nonmonetary ways to express your appreciation. You're getting education in the most personalized form there is.

- **Contracts with experts.** (C) "I've got a guy for that." These are people who advise you individually or as part of a board of advisers, offering guidance in a particular area of expertise and opening doors to opportunity.

- **Formal board of directors.** (A) At this level, you have elected to hold your organization to a higher level of control than your own leadership, one that both offers guidance and keeps you accountable as CEO.

- **Executive management courses.** (T) There are many university- and consultancy-based programs in executive education, and they come in various types and lengths. These are "real" school, with curricula, homework, presentations, and, often, graduation ceremonies.

Whatever your choice(s), "school" has plenty to teach you.

Begin with the end in mind. Your job as founder/entrepreneur/ CEO is to raise the value of your business—and that stock certificate is right there at the beginning of your QE Notebook, staring at you. As your business grows, so does your responsibility to ensure the future of not just the enterprise, but of the people who have joined you and bought into your vision and energy with their commitment of time. Who do you want them to see when they look at you as leader? Somebody who thinks they've got it all together and has nothing to learn? Or somebody who shows by example that continuous improvement applies to the boss as well as to the business?

CHAPTER 11 QUAL CARD

Initial each requirement as met:

PREREQUISITES

The entrepreneur has become fully self-aware that "I don't know what I don't know" (IDKWIDK), and that it's better to achieve a status of "I know what I don't know" (IKWIDK). This self-knowledge has revealed how the entrepreneur's short-comings may be affecting his/her company and has resulted in a commitment to a lifelong learning process.

The entrepreneur has developed his/her Entrepreneurial Education Lifeline and overlaid it with the Career/Professional Lifeline created early in the book, looking for any "aha moments" that may be observed in his/her career to date. Both have been extended out three to five years in the future.

The entrepreneur has committed to
increasing his/her personal capacity. To
that end, he/she has listed the entrepreneurial education methods to be utilized
in the next 12 months (choosing from the
Accountability, Consultation, and Teaching
options listed in this chapter).   _____

SIGNATURE: _____

DATE: _____

CHAPTER 12

BOR-E-GAGED

"I hate it when people call themselves 'entrepreneurs'
when what they're really trying to do is launch a
startup and then...cash in and move on. They're
unwilling to do the work it takes to build a real
company, which is the hardest work in business.

—STEVE JOBS

I love to hear entrepreneurs comparing notes on how many businesses they've started. It gets to be a form of one-upmanship.

"I've started two."

"Well, I've started four."

"My fifth launches this spring."

So, what's your count? One? Three? Ten? I've been part of five startups. Yet I still have to fight the urge to unfavorably compare myself to somebody who's started more.

When I was a young and IDKWIDK kind of entrepreneur, I thought starting businesses was something you had to do to maintain your entrepreneurial cred. It was a drive and a duty,

I believed. It's what any card-carrying entrepreneur should be unable to *avoid* doing, in fact! Add another startup to your résumé, add another ribbon to your shoulder. I also kept count of how many employees I had hired and the number of offices I had opened—the more the better. It reminds me of a pop/rock song someone quoted to me awhile back: "Too much of anything is never enough (give me more, give me more.)" ("Love etc.," by Pet Shop Boys.)[1]

If you're keeping track as you read this book, you're now wondering about Business Five, because thus far I've only mentioned four businesses—two of which were merged into one in 1996. Well, the company I haven't talked about yet is actually number two on the list, chronologically, and it's time to tell its story.

THE BOR-E-GAGED TRAP

My partners and I were about three years into our first business when the urge struck me to start another one. At that point Business One, Orion International, was making money, achieving steady employment growth, and starting to pay the owners a decent salary. Not knowing much of anything about what it was going to take to grow the first business to peak revenues and profits, I found myself a little bored.

> I think of entrepreneurial attention span as a short continuum that stretches from bored to engaged.

Let me pause here and expand the definition for the title of this chapter, "bor-e-gaged." I think of entrepreneurial attention span as a short continuum that stretches from bored to engaged. And my made-up word for being stuck smack in the middle, or vacillating frequently from left to right in the middle zone, is "bor-e-gaged"—a little of each.

Bor-e-gaged is an uncomfortable place to be. You're not engaged enough to truly focus on the business you're operating, and you're not mind-numbingly bored enough to cut the cord and move on. In the middle zone, you're not putting the effort into something new yet—but you're thinking about it, and your current company is suffering from your lack of engagement.

So that's where I was when I began daydreaming about Business Two—I was bobbing around in bor-e-gaged territory. On the one hand, I regarded Orion with pride and satisfaction and loved every minute of being part of it. On the other, I missed the excitement I felt when it was a true startup. I saw entrepreneurs around me moving on to their Business Two, and I felt anxious to catch up. As I said above, it just felt like what entrepreneurs should do. They start businesses, right? They don't just sit there and become …*CEOs*.

I didn't perceive any real risk in launching something new. I didn't see how starting a new company could hurt Orion. Being the Ever Optimistic sort of personality that I was at the time, it didn't occur to me that anything could go wrong. In fact, despite being darned busy with Business One, it didn't even cross my mind that I might be stretched too thin. "I can bring somebody in to build it," I told myself, when thinking of managing Business Two. "I'll just provide the vision, and offer up a little guidance now and then, and it'll be off and running." The desire to believe myself was strong. Getting Business Two going would give me another notch in my entrepreneurial belt, earning new respect from my fellow entrepreneurs, and making Mom and Dad proud all over again.

It was a bad move, as I'm sure you've already figured out. I hired an Operations person, basically telling him to take my concept and run with it. He looked at me like I was nuts. Where were the operating manuals, the SOPs (standard operating procedures), etc.? How would he know what to do 1st, 2nd, and 15th? Well, crud. I thought it would all just happen. The experience taught me that having good ideas is great, but success is in the execution— as well as in the focus the entrepreneur gives to the business.

Having the right people in the right seats does matter, and I learned that lesson in spades with Business Two. The Ops guy was the right guy in the wrong seat, or at least at the wrong time. The business failed, and I have only myself to blame. It wasn't anybody's fault but mine that I wasn't willing or able to give the business sufficient attention.

> The business failed, and I have only myself to blame. It wasn't anybody's fault but mine that I wasn't willing or able to give the business sufficient attention.

For most of us, bor-e-gage-ment ebbs and flows, but it never really goes away. I felt the startup urge again like crazy in 1999, when the dot-com era was at its peak. Entrepreneurs were starting online businesses pretty much at the click of a mouse and selling them for huge amounts of money. It was *the norm* to do this, leaving those of us who weren't doing the same feeling like slackers or fools. Sitting there at the Birthing of Giants program with 60 other entrepreneurs, most of whom could claim a dot-com startup or two, I felt hopelessly out of step. How could I call myself an entrepreneur if I wasn't a *serial* entrepreneur, driven to start one business after another? Why wasn't I cashing in on the Internet trend? Looking back, of course I'm glad I didn't go down that path, because the eventual dot-com crash took the dreams of many entrepreneurs down with it.

Bor-e-gagement is fraught with risk, folks—for everybody it touches. It's a virus that can't be killed but must be controlled. And we entrepreneurs do that mostly by acknowledging the power it has over us. I'm not saying serial entrepreneurship is bad, because it isn't. Boredom combined with a real, exploitable opportunity can lead to great success. **It's serial entrepreneurship for the *sake* of serial entrepreneurship that's bad, especially when our exits or distractions harm the businesses we've already started.**

See if you can find yourself below. Our differing CEO personalities see serial startups in ways that are characteristic of our world views:

Urgent/Reactive: For this fire-ready-aim personality, the attitude toward new ventures is, "Just start 'em up and see what happens." This entrepreneur absolutely loves to be busy—in fact, the busier the better, because to him or her, busy means successful. Will there be disasters and conflagrations? Sure! And this go-getter will be only too happy to come in as first responder, sirens wailing. That's what this personality lives for, and bor-e-gagement provides plenty of it.

Ever Optimistic: Again, for this individual (as it is for Urgent/ Reactive), it's the more the merrier where startups are concerned. In fact, this entrepreneur fully expects to be measured by the number of businesses he or she has started. Having been this person, I can clearly recall sort of beating my chest whenever I was asked how many startups I'd had. I was actually offended if someone assumed I'd had only one! The internal monologue, which I well remember, goes like this: "There's no end to my ideas, and my ideas lead to companies!" In fact, I have a hunch that perhaps Ever Optimistic types, as a group, are the true serial entrepreneurs—the ones with two, three, five, or more startups to their name—simply because they are so naturally optimistic. With their can-do spirit, they're the ones who actually bring to fruition the ideas that other personality types think of but don't act upon. If this describes you, you are a rarity and should be celebrated for all you do. But the rest of this chapter will give you some interesting questions to ponder.

Reflexively Pessimistic: Since this personality will choose any port in a storm, always seeking and waiting for calmer seas, serial entrepreneurship doesn't come easily to this group. The attitude is, "I'm not going to venture far because there's trouble lurking around every corner." New companies will be started by this type of entrepreneur, but never without thought and reflection—and great self-doubt.

Steady/Proactive: Ideally, we entrepreneurs shouldn't be starting companies just to start companies. I think we should all strive to think, *"It's not the number of companies I start; it's how they do over time. I start companies to build valuable, market-leading enterprises that last."* Steady/Proactive takes into account the realities of market dynamics and financing and labor—and all the rest—and blends it with optimism (and luck, if we're honest about it) to make good bets on the future.

Bor-e-gagement has the potential to strike any or all of us, regardless of personality type. For anyone in that zone, the idea of starting a new business is a thrilling thought, but putting in the long hours and hard work to build the long-term success of a business already up and running is . . . *boring.* So we either scramble things in our existing company in the name of change or we give in to the virus and turn our energy toward creating a new company. The prospect of doing something new is magnetic in its pull. Choosing instead to stay engaged with the existing enterprise, Business One, takes a kind of focus and willpower—and yes, strength—that not many of us easily find.

To many of us, managing for operational excellence and business longevity doesn't sound appealing. Using a parenting analogy, it's like the relentless work of raising a child as opposed to the joy following the child's birth. We all know that we can't bail out on the kid when the going gets tough. So, why do we entrepreneurs let ourselves think we can start up a company and leave it when it's become less fun? In building businesses as in raising children, there is simply no substitute for focus and hard work over the long haul. If you want my point of view in a nutshell, it's this:

It may be in my nature and yours to want to start companies one after another, but over time I have come to see that the impulse to do serial startups is a little wet behind the ears. My matured self now tells me to grow *better* companies, not just more of them. This is what *Qualified* Entrepreneurs do well.

I want to see more *Qualified* Entrepreneurs building disciplined entrepreneurial companies and giving them the same "roots and wings" we try to build into our children before we turn them loose in the world.

Remember the Small Business Administration statistics:[2, 3]

> I want to see more *Qualified* Entrepreneurs building disciplined entrepreneurial companies and giving them the same "roots and wings" we try to build into our children before we turn them loose in the world.

• 50 percent of businesses fail in the first 5 years.

• 70 percent of businesses are out of business within 10 years.

I started five businesses and, as you've learned, one failed because I was unable to turn my back on the siren's song calling me to start a new business. But after that episode, I got much more serious about adding discipline to my entrepreneurial toolkit, and I morphed my leadership personality from Urgent/Reactive to something closer to Steady/Proactive (suffering my share of sunburns and storms from my Ever Optimistic and Reflexively

Pessimistic periods along the way). I became a *Qualified* Entrepreneur, and I wish the same for you and others.

Encouraging entrepreneurs to deal effectively with their bor-e-gagement is a crucial step, I believe, toward reducing the business failure rate. But that doesn't mean I'm in favor of stifling our entrepreneurial instincts; I just want to see them better harnessed and put to work for us, instead of running away with us. I'm arguing for each of us to embrace the responsibility we have to our existing businesses, whether they are in the fast growth phase, or struggling to survive. I'm arguing, as always, for self-awareness. We need to recognize the difference between boredom and active engagement so that we can *manage ourselves* appropriately for the good of our companies and their future. In the latter 1990s, when

> We need to recognize the difference between boredom and active engagement so that we can *manage ourselves* appropriately for the good of our companies and their future.

my business was growing wildly and I was in the mood to start more companies, I heard business coach and consultant (and now friend) Rich Russakoff say, *"You have no idea now, but it is going to take 100 percent of your effort to make just one business run well over time."* It didn't fully resonate with me then, but I remembered it. In hindsight, I see it as one of the best bits of wisdom I've ever received.

So ask yourself: **How many ships can you captain at the same time? No, let me rephrase that. How many ships can you captain *well*—especially in rough seas?**

I captained two ships, one for 14 years and the other for 10. You'll note the past tense there, but it doesn't mean I didn't follow my own guidance. On the contrary, it was becoming a *Qualified Entrepreneur* that led me to face and make the Second Decision (to support and create at Orion and NSTAR, respectively). It was the preparation I gave myself that helped me to recognize when the time was right to relinquish the bridge to other captains.

> In a *Fortune* magazine article from 2012, business experts gauged the optimal tenure for successful CEOs—both for the CEOs themselves and for their companies, that is—to be 10 to 15 years.

Judging by research on the subject of CEO tenure, my exit timing was about right. In a *Fortune* magazine article from 2012, business experts gauged the optimal tenure for successful CEOs—both for the CEOs themselves and for their companies, that is—to be 10 to 15 years.[4] Think about why this is true: After 10 to 15 years, you're likely to have experienced a few economic cycles, riding the wave up, then down, then up again. After that kind of strategic workout, how many of us feel equipped and excited to ride out two or three more cycles in the same boat? How many of us will be able to turn the bow into the waves with real zeal, knowing how rough it's going to be? Might somebody else at the helm be a better choice?

This is a question we all answer for ourselves based on as much discipline as we can bring to the decision. Stepping aside *could* be the right answer for you, if:

- … your real skill is starting companies, not building them, and both you and your employees know it. (Remember, becoming a Creator is a valid choice for any *Qualified* Entrepreneur, as you'll see when it comes time to fill out your final Qual Card and make the Second Decision!)

- … you aren't disciplined about managing; you make decisions on a wing and a prayer.

- … you actively forgo the systematic development of operational excellence and allow yourself to become captivated by new ideas.

- … you are burned out and lack the energy to give the position the 100 percent focused effort necessary to meet the company's needs and true capabilities.

- … you think more about opportunities to be exploited and money to be made than customers to be served and employees hired.

If some or all of these sound like you, you're either getting bored or you're not the kind of entrepreneur who is cut out to find engagement in company building. But as you're reaching for the doorknob, I'd invite you to weigh one more factor: your employees. Think of how they have come to trust your leadership to keep them employed and reasonably prosperous. How many of them have mortgages or rent to pay, kids to raise, or health issues to manage (with the help of your company health plan)? I'm not saying you can't move on to new adventures—you can. But if you haven't been a *Qualified* Entrepreneur, one who has put in the time and effort to build a disciplined company, then you are essentially saying to the people in the office or factory, "Good luck! I'm jumping ship in search of new and exciting opportunities. I have done what I can do here, and it's time for me to move on and do what I do best—which is starting companies and getting new people excited about my latest vision." Don't do that to your loyal employees, at least not without answering these two crucial questions:

- Is the company in good hands? Is there a CEO running it, someone who is trained and has cleared something akin to a Qual Card process to ensure readiness?

- Do you have the company set up for success with a clear vision and goals and plans in place?

If you can think about jumping ship without fearing for your employees' future, and if you feel confident in the leader or team of managers who will succeed you, maybe it *is* the right time to give in to your boredom or follow your creative instincts to the next opportunity.

With the guidance of a final Qual Card at the end of this book, you may elect to use your new status as a *Qualified* Entrepreneur to continue to lead as the CEO, to support from a non-CEO role, or to create anew, perhaps from outside the existing company. Which role would I love to see you choose? Any of the three will work, since they all lead to an increase in **Qualified** Entrepreneurs leading or supporting their organizations or creating new disciplined organizations . . . a win-win-win across the board!

I'll end the chapter with the equation that guides me—and the one I believe should guide all of us:

Entrepreneurial energy + Lifelong learning + Disciplined thinking and execution = Improved performance and reduced failure rate

If you get bored (and we all do at some point), engage yourself *or someone else* to keep the ship on course for a long and successful future.

CHAPTER 12 QUAL CARD

Initial each requirement as met:

PREREQUISITES	INITIALS
The entrepreneur has determined where he/she falls on the bored/engaged scale and why.	_____
The entrepreneur has assessed his/her leadership personality (Urgent/Reactive, Ever Optimistic, Reflexively Pessimistic, or Steady/Proactive) with regard to serial entrepreneurship and bor-e-gagement.	_____
The entrepreneur has reviewed the businesses that he/she has started, and has evaluated how bor-e-gagement prompted startups of new companies or contributed to business failures.	_____
The entrepreneur has conducted the self-examination necessary to determine whether he/she is running the current business for the benefit of an entrepreneurial ego or for the long-term success of the company and its employees.	_____

The entrepreneur has developed a list of actions that would need to be taken to ready his/her current business for a transition to new leadership, should he/she elect to move on to a new startup. _____

SIGNATURE: _____

DATE: _____

CHAPTER 13

CRISIS LEADERSHIP, CONTINGENCY PLANNING AND THE RESET BUTTON

"There's no harm in hoping for the best as long as you're prepared for the worst."

—STEPHEN KING, *DIFFERENT SEASONS*

In the US Navy, training happens all the time. This is intentional, so that sailors will find it second nature to work at the problem and truly perform should an actual emergency arise. In my last three months of pre-submarine schooling, I spent time in various types of mechanical trainers, including ones that would simulate fire, flood, and the dreaded "jam dive." That's when you head straight for the bottom of the ocean because the submarine's steering mechanism is stuck in the "down" position. It's sort of like speeding 70 miles per hour in a car with a stuck brake pedal and a cliff looming a mile or two ahead. It's, *uh*, exhilarating—especially the first time you experience it.

But the training didn't stop when the schooling did. On average, most days we spent multiple hours in drills when we were aboard the submarine. We would go through many of the same routines that we did in the trainers, plus simulating other emergencies and, of course, practicing various scenarios that would require us to deploy weapons or defend ourselves from attack. If there was a scenario that could be imagined, there was a drill for it. In this way, crisis became "normal" for us. We learned to expect trouble and feel confident that we had a protocol to handle it. We proved to ourselves over and over again that we could operate the submarine in just about any condition, and keep it operating, whatever the situation. Knowing what to do kept us calm and ready to act.

> If there was a scenario that could be imagined, there was a drill for it. In this way, crisis became "normal" for us. We learned to expect trouble and feel confident that we had a protocol to handle it.

The genius of US Navy training, however, is that it teaches a sailor not just to respond to trouble, but to truly *expect* it. This is especially necessary for sailors on submarines, where maintaining the proper environment is critical. Survival itself depends on preventing even tiny changes in oxygen levels and water pressure and avoiding fire and steam leaks at all costs. Think about food in the microwave oven and the steam that's released when you remove the plastic wrap—then multiply that steam and its pressure hundreds of times and that's what a potential steam leak would create on a submarine! The drills teach you to accept that bad things can and likely will happen. The US Navy knows that you need to *take the fear out of the emergency*—and then train the brain to take the right steps in the right order. That's how you survive.

While working on this chapter, I happened to read about an intriguing study, one that not only validates the sort of training the military does, but explains how and why it works. Psychologists at the University of California, San Diego, monitored the brain activity of a varied group of study participants—battle-trained Marines, competitive athletes, and regular folks—as they completed cognitive tasks. The researchers added stress to the experience by occasionally restricting airflow to the masks the participants were wearing, making it hard for them to breathe. Some participants couldn't stand the "aversive stimulus," panicked, and left the study. But the others, mostly Marines and athletes, adapted quickly.[1]

Here's what interested me: the participants in this study didn't know when their breathing would become difficult, but after a few experiences with restricted oxygen, researchers could tell that the group knew it was coming. How? By seeing changes in the subjects' brains via MRI imaging. Just before the airflow was restricted, these individuals, well-trained by their careers, showed higher activation in the insular cortex of the brain. They were preparing themselves for the expected discomfort. Then, almost as soon as the restricted airflow began, the same region of the brain went back to business as usual. Said researcher Martin Paulus, "That kind of anticipation and preparation is critical" to human success in challenging circumstances—whether it's coming under enemy fire, needing to correct for a badly timed mistake in an athletic contest, or responding to any other situation that requires quick, calm action. He says it's crucial to train your brain to anticipate and react without overreacting. The title of the blog entry in which I read about the study was "Anticipating the Strain."[2]

What a perfect analogy for the contingency planning and crisis leadership I'm advocating in this chapter!

Think of the Urgent/Reactive leader that I've described throughout this book, the one that most of us have embodied at one time or another. This person is all about impulse and speed, putting out those proverbial fires as they break out and quickly moving on to the next, always thriving on the chaos. As I've pointed out, it's not the best model for competent leadership. Compare him or her to Steady/Proactive, the kind of leader we all should hope to become. The difference is Steady/Proactive's ability to expect trouble and plan ahead for a calm and effective response. In other words, the difference between the types is *discipline*—the kind I advocate in entrepreneurial business, which is much like the kind the US Navy instilled in me as an officer. As an entrepreneur, however, I have had to teach the discipline to myself . . . and almost always at times when it would have helped to have known it already!

DISRUPTION WILL HAPPEN

Let me briefly discuss with you two significant "crises" I've experienced with business disruption. In both cases, I credit my military training and experience for keeping me as calm and focused as possible. Just as in the US Navy, I knew that there was no option but to survive—and the quicker I could get to work on solving the problem(s), the better.

You'll recall that my first company, Orion International, was founded in 1991 to place military veterans in civilian-sector jobs. Business was great—phenomenal, really—until the 9/11 attacks occurred in 2001, throwing the country into an economic downturn. Both our supply of labor *and* the demand for it evaporated within a matter of weeks. The military's post-9/11 "stop-loss" policies kept select military personnel from separating from the services or retiring, so we suddenly had a significantly lower percentage of the armed forces to place into jobs. At the same time, demand collapsed as companies elected to sit tight on hiring and wait for the economy to shake off its shell-shock. So there we were, having just expanded the company to meet increased demand for the hard and soft skills our veterans bring to the marketplace, only to watch our contracts almost totally dry up. The result was painful downsizing, transforming what had been a multimillion dollar company into a shadow of its former self—a shadow close to 25 percent the size of its former self. It was soul-crushing. But what choice did I have if I wanted the company to survive?

My second business, NSTAR Global, has a similar crisis story, but it ended better—thanks to the discipline I acquired after the earlier crisis at Orion. Beginning in 2007, NSTAR's industry (semiconductors) underwent structural changes that took its equipment sector from an annual volume of over $40 billion per year to less than $15 billion. Ouch. The contraction took about two years— and lucky for me, I'd made the right bet and found myself sitting pretty when the market finally rebounded. But I wouldn't have made it to the "sitting pretty" point if I hadn't known how to respond quickly and competently to preserve the business's cash, and with it, its profitability.

Are you reading along, thinking that these sorts of changes won't affect your company? That your business is unlikely to be affected by the sorts of disruptions that my companies suffered through? Well, let's play the "good old days" game and see what's different now than it was just 24 years ago (that's not that many years!) when I started my entrepreneurial career:

Politics: We've been through Presidents George H. W. Bush, Bill Clinton, George W. Bush, and Barack Obama, with many differences in policy, style, and substance.

History: End of the Soviet Union. First Gulf War. War in Bosnia. Genocide in Rwanda. The end of apartheid in South Africa. Massive business restructuring and reinvestment in preparation for what became known as "Y2K." Mad Cow disease in Europe. Climate change. Uprisings in the Middle East and Africa. And, of course, the attacks of 9/11 that sent us to war in Iraq and Afghanistan—not to mention various earthquakes and a cataclysmic tsunami affecting 11 countries.

Economy: We had a short recession in 1990–1991, rebounding with a major economic expansion in the Clinton and dot-com years. We struggled through another brief recession in 2001 (which economists say may not have occurred if we hadn't had the 9/11 attacks). Finally, the Great Recession occurred, caused by the financial crisis. It is recognized as the worst downturn since the Great Depression, and technically occurred from December 2007 to June 2009. However, as most of us know, it had a depressive effect on employment and business growth well beyond its supposed end.

Technology: Change here has been revolutionary. Desktop computers, which are still ubiquitous but quickly being replaced by tablets and smartphones, were by no means common in the early 1990s. My first business started without desktops. The World Wide Web, invented in 1989, existed only for nerds and geeks. (We called them "systems majors" in college in the 1980s, and now they're technology entrepreneurs!) All of us carried credit cards that allowed us to make mobile calls from phone booths and airport concourses, where long lines of business people often awaited their turn. Now, of course, both communications and computing are completely mobile, and a growing volume of business is conducted exclusively online. Ask newspapers, magazines, and record companies if the internet improved their business or not. Ask folks at Microsoft if they think Google has gained any ground on them since 1991. Ask dictators and governments around the world if Facebook and Twitter have had any impact on civil unrest in their countries. And just try imagining what your own children or grandchildren will consider "normal" 25 years from now!

Having taken this trip down memory lane, stop now and consider the massive change that could be just around the corner for *you and your company*. Ask yourself: "Will I be ready?"

Your answer to the above question almost has to be "no." As entrepreneurs, we operate from a philosophy that the glass is . . . forget half, to us that glass is always three-quarters full. We think that revenues and profits always grow and that adversity only strikes *other* companies. This attitude comes from our lack of training (discipline) combined with our tendency toward an overabundance of self-confidence.

PREPARE YOUR BUSINESS FOR INEVITABLE SETBACKS

But remember the statistics: Entrepreneurial businesses *do* fail up to 50 percent of the time at the 5-year mark, and up to 70 percent of the time 10 years out—even businesses that surprise us, that make magazine covers and beauty-contest lists.[3, 4] No one is invulnerable. Our gung-ho attitude won't inoculate us against threats such as unmanaged growth or debilitating economic downturns. Nor will it stave off the kind of disruption that your competitors are just itching to cause you in any way they can! What will your business and your industry look like if and when those competitors are successful?

Just as training improves outcomes in the US Navy, anticipation—along with careful planning that is guided by a vision and followed up with well-led execution of plans—*can* save a company from its own versions of fire, flood, and attack. I know, because I've lived it; I've watched CEO-friends struggle through it (painfully but mostly successfully). So I'm confident in saying that if you haven't experienced a serious setback in your business yet, statistics indicate that you likely will, and maybe soon. Maybe the competition will catch you, or your product will become commoditized, or the economy will tank and drag you down with it, or your patent will expire with nothing else in the pipeline, or . . . something. No matter what business you are in, no matter how winning your product or strategic advantage may be, you will someday find yourself countering the equivalent of a submarine's jam dive to survive.

So what is your protocol? What do you do first, second, and third when a crisis hits?

In my opinion, the protocol starts, ends, and centers on COGS— cost of goods sold. We've talked about COGS in detail, and to my way of thinking, it's the manual not just for *running* a disciplined business, as we discussed back then, but also for *saving* one. **COGS helps you figure out how to make money at *any* revenue level.** And this has to be your task when trouble starts—staying profitable and preserving cash, and thereby staying in business.

That's tough for most of us. We entrepreneurs are all about growth. We'll do anything to avoid downsizing—including going out of business, it sometimes seems! But the truth is, if you manage to keep dropping even a small amount of money to the bottom line, you stay in business. Let me show you. Here's the chart from the COGS-nizance chapter, revised. It assumes that you've already elevated your expenses to the levels anticipated for $5 million in revenue. But everything's gone sour, and a more realistic revenue number is now $3 million, which is now entered where the $5 million used to be. Look at what happens:

	2012	2013	2014	BUDGET 2015	ACTUAL 2015	%'s 2012	%'s 2013	%'s 2014	BUDGET Target %'s 2015	ACTUAL 2015	RESET Target %	RESET Expenses	VARIANCE (from budget)
Revenue	3500000	4250000	4500000	5000000	3000000	3500000	4250000	4500000	5000000	3000000	3000000	3000000	
Expenses													
Rent	350000	350000	375000	425000	425000	10.00%	8.24%	8.33%	8.50%	14.17%	12.00%	360000	-65000
Office Supplies	14750	15000	16750	17000	17000	0.42%	0.35%	0.37%	0.34%	0.57%	0.40%	12000	-5000
Payroll	1530000	2050000	2250000	2650000	2650000	43.71%	48.24%	50.00%	53.00%	88.33%	67.50%	2025000	-625000
Legal	25000	15000	40000	25000	25000	0.71%	0.35%	0.89%	0.50%	0.83%	0.60%	18000	-7000
Accounting	17500	17500	18000	18000	18000	0.50%	0.41%	0.40%	0.36%	0.60%	0.47%	14100	-3900
Depreciation	10000	10000	10000	10000	10000	0.29%	0.24%	0.22%	0.20%	0.33%	0.30%	9000	-1000
Travel	30000	50000	50000	60000	60000	0.86%	1.18%	1.11%	1.20%	2.00%	1.50%	45000	-15000
Meals	3500	3400	3600	4000	4000	0.10%	0.08%	0.08%	0.08%	0.13%	0.10%	3000	-1000
Computer	2500	2500	2750	27520	27520	0.07%	0.06%	0.06%	0.55%	0.92%	0.07%	2100	-25420
Marketing	10000	75000	50000	100000	100000	0.29%	1.76%	1.11%	2.00%	3.33%	2.06%	61800	-38200
Miscellaneous	500000	600000	650000	675000	675000	14.29%	14.12%	14.44%	13.50%	22.50%	15.00%	450000	-225000
Total Expenses	2493250	3188400	3466100	4011520	4011520	71.24%	75.02%	77.02%	80.23%	133.72%	100.00%	3000000	-1011520
Profit	1006750	1061600	1033900	988480	-1011520								
Profit %	28.76%	24.98%	22.98%	19.77%	-33.72%	28.76%	24.98%	22.98%	19.77%	-33.72%	0.00%		

Your profit takes a hit, as expected. But look what happens to your COGS numbers—wow!

Below is the to-do list I suggest for crisis management. These are the steps you need to take, in my opinion, to keep your ship safely underway even when the worst storm hits. If you are the CEO or operate at a CEO-level of responsibility, this list is your protocol, your discipline:

1. Get your COGS report up to date, as shown in the chart above. It should contain three years of history, your target percentages, and for comparison, your percentages for the current fiscal year. (See Chapters 8 and 9 for review.)

2. Determine your current projected revenue level. In the case of the example, it is now $3 million instead of the budgeted $5 million.

3. Get your critical decision makers in a room and work the rest of the list together.

4. Set the acceptable profit/loss percentage at which you are willing to operate the business for the current fiscal year. This is a critical discussion and decision, because you are (1) committing to lead the business past this crisis and (2) setting the standard for financial operations moving forward. (For the example, I have chosen to break even, 0% profit for the year, so I can retain as many of my valued employees as possible.)

5. Set your target COGS percentages for each expense category. The total when added up should equal the profit/loss percentage target.

6. Create a new column that will calculate the new expense number that is acceptable for revenue of $3 million, and in the next column create a variance between the current expense numbers (based on the $5 million budget) and the proposed expense targets for the newly expected revenue of $3 million.

7. Challenge the notion that fixed costs must be fixed. The one that comes to mind first is your lease exposure. In our case, when we had to hit the reset button, we had nine offices and annual lease agreements. In the end, we subleased a handful of them. Fixed costs skyrocket in terms of COGS percentages when revenue plummets, so put them on the discussion table and get to work coming up with ideas on how to reduce them, and quickly.

8. With the big picture now in mind, get to work on each expense category. Decide how you will get from current levels to where you need to be. Remember that the cuts need to be made to preserve cash and future profit potential. You can't accept losses that will endanger your company's ongoing operation. You will see in the example the brutal, unfortunate facts, which are that you need to cut $1,011,520 in expenses, and $625,000 of it will be in personnel costs.

9. Lastly, don't let any of your team leave the room until there's a survival plan in place and general agreement reached that this is the plan that will keep the company in business. Confidence is the key here.

Now you know what you'll do if the bottom falls out. The principles of COGS and COGS percentages allow you to compare expenditures at various revenue levels to help you to rapidly confront reality when it's most important to do so. Read the list a few times—both to get a feel for what you'd need to do in an emergency and to take some of the panic out of it. In this way you will be "Anticipating the Strain," just like the test subjects did when their brains prepared for oxygen deprivation.[5] Try answering some of the questions you'll need to address if and when this day arrives. Consider it your drill. Get comfortable enough that, again, like the research subjects, your brain will actually quiet down when "go time" arrives, allowing you to work the problem like the *Qualified* Entrepreneur that you are.

Of course, preparing and practicing the protocols is only half the battle, as we've said. You need to expect trouble and anticipate its origin. Before we move on, try this: write down the top 10 reasons why your company could suffer a reduction in revenues of 25 percent or more.

    1.

    2.

    3.

    4.

    5.

    6.

    7.

    8.

    9.

    10.

If you had difficulty coming up with 10 possibilities for disruptive change, well, it may be that you suffer from a lack of imagination! Or, as Jim Collins and Morten T. Hansen, authors of *Great by Choice: Uncertainty, Chaos, and Luck—Why Some Thrive Despite Them All,* might put it, where's your "productive paranoia?"[6] (To Collins and Hansen, productive paranoia involves obsessing—in good times and bad—about what can go wrong, planning for catastrophe, and thriving in uncertainty.) So check your card: Aren't entrepreneurs like us supposed to be able to see opportunity almost everywhere—and maybe *especially* in disruptions that alter a marketplace? Shouldn't we be comfortable imagining scenarios by which our old way of doing business would give way to something newer and maybe even quite different . . . but profitable nonetheless? Aren't innovation and creativity critical in both good times and bad?

I think so, and that's why I'm so fond of the concept of the RESET button. I want to spend some of the rest of this chapter talking about why each of us should quit avoiding the darn thing and, when necessary, push it decisively.

Aren't entrepreneurs like us supposed to be able to see opportunity almost everywhere— and maybe *especially* in disruptions that alter a marketplace?

WHEN SHOULD YOU PUSH THE RESET BUTTON?

This requires some retraining of instincts, of course. The RESET button that most of us know best is right there on the computer's CPU, and it's the thing you don't even want your fingers to brush against—because if you inadvertently push the button, everything you've ever known will be gone. You will be forced to create something new, and no matter how much you may want it to be the same, it will be different. For many of us, this is a scary feeling. But I've come to think of the RESET button as a *necessary tool* for the *Qualified* Entrepreneur. Used properly, it's a fresh start and a way to ensure that your company avoids becoming part of those much-publicized entrepreneurial failure rates.

My definition of the term: A RESET button is a tool for the entrepreneur to utilize during significant downturns or disruptions that require reorganization, downsizing, layoffs, or all of the above.

The RESET button works best when pushed firmly. Used late or half-heartedly, it doesn't work as it should. If the RESET isn't used at all, the entrepreneur or CEO is voting to maintain the status quo—which can be comforting to the leader, but fatal to a company that is under significant stress. By being unwilling to accept and deal with the change that has been thrust upon the company, the entrepreneur or CEO has guaranteed the company nothing but more quarters of poor performance. It's like knowing a Category 2 hurricane is coming (which sounds minor, but, knowing the scale as I do from living in North Carolina, isn't)— yet staying put, hoping for the best. That's a guaranteed disaster!

> The highest and best use of the RESET button is, to me, *keeping the company alive for the people who are still in it instead of letting it die for the employees you couldn't stand to lose or the markets your pride wouldn't let you abandon.*

Pushing the RESET button isn't a cop-out or a failure—far from it. The highest and best use of the RESET button is, to me, *keeping the company alive for the people who are still in it instead of letting it die for the employees you couldn't stand to lose or the markets your pride wouldn't let you abandon.* The entrepreneurial ego is a beautiful and powerful thing—until it prevents us from doing what should be done. So don't resist. When circumstances warrant it, push the button. You will want to second-guess yourself; you shouldn't. Everything within you will argue against downsizing and finding a fresh start, but don't listen. Having observed my own reactions and those of others confronting the RESET button over the years, I can safely predict that these are the battles you'll face:

- You will think, "I can't cut my costs any more." I say that's absolutely untrue, and completing the COGS exercise in the preceding section should make you a believer. I have helped more peers than I would have liked do the same. As I told them, I wasn't any smarter than them; it just happened to me first. And experience put me in a position to help them weather the storm.

- You will try to slow or minimize your downsizing, hoping that the crisis is temporary and that you'll soon be posting growth again. But in the end, you may learn what I did—it's better to go deeper and quicker with your cuts instead of procrastinating.

- You will try to hold onto good people for as long as possible, and if you fail you will immediately begin trying to bring them back. Don't do either. You *will* lose good people, you *must*, and it will tear you apart.

I remember feeling that I had let our employees down, even though everything that had occurred was well out of my control. Looking them in the eyes and telling them that I didn't have a place for them anymore, simply because the business wasn't performing well enough—well, I don't think I can express how difficult it was. But, with hindsight, I can see that the best plan is to face the ugly reality and make the cuts. Don't gear your new plans toward trying to rehire your lost employees, either. Focus instead on the new people who will join your company after the crisis is over, bringing fresh perspectives. Let the people who lost their trust in you and your company find a new sense of security somewhere else. It's good for them, and it's also going to be what's best for your company's future.

- You will want to believe that your culture can survive unaffected by the crisis—but it can't, at least for the time being. For as long as the crisis persists and maybe longer, yours is no longer a growth company. Lead well, and you may bring back the go-go years. But you can't let yourself be fooled into thinking that nothing has changed.

- In the heat of battle, you may begin to lose sight of your core values. Remind yourself of them. Does it alter who you are when you change your look (with new clothes, new hairstyle, or weight loss)? No, and it should be no different for your company. Remember the 4 Cs from the Values-Based Leadership chapter of this book: Change, Controversy, Crisis, and—this last one is the relevant one for this chapter—Courage.[7, 8, 9] You need to have the courage to right your ship when your company and its people are relying on you to do it, and the best way to do it without sacrificing your core values is to utilize the RESET button.

- You might feel ashamed in front of your employees and peers. Fight the feeling. Instead, you must adjust to your new revenue level and . . . take pride in knowing that you are living a survival story and laying the groundwork for your future successful business. You are still afloat! You did not go to zero! Think of how many of your CEO peers aren't doing as well. Think, too, of how many new entrepreneurs would be thrilled to have a $4 million company—or even $2 million or $1 million, if that's how low it goes.

- You will be tempted to label yourself a failure. You are not. You failed only in this moment, and for reasons that were likely beyond your control. Your company has taken a hit, but it is not dead. Entrepreneurs who want to build companies and be the CEO need to understand that difficult times do happen, and, boy oh boy, these are actually the perfect times to learn lessons and acquire more discipline.

Ideally, a crisis significant enough to make your business a smaller version of itself . . . will make its leader a *smarter* version of himself or herself. It was certainly true for me. I've used the fresh start represented by pushing the RESET button to take a look at my metrics, and you should do the same. Are they the right ones? Might you avoid future business disruption by adding new metrics or eliminating some old, ineffective ones that distract you from seeing where your business is really headed? I also recommend that you add a macroeconomic component to your three-year vision, if you didn't have one before. If your business disruption was the result of an industry-wide condition or change, this is crucial. You need to learn how the industry dragged your company down to a new reality, why it happened, how long it will last, and how you can spot trouble next time, preferably before it really arrives. Remember Collins and Hansen: a little productive paranoia can be a very good thing. Besides, you really don't have long to put off your future-casting: in the final chapter of the book, as part of making your Second Decision, I'll be asking you to forecast your business timeline out three to five years, taking into consideration the future of your industry.

> Ideally, a crisis significant enough to make your business a smaller version of itself ... will make its leader a *smarter* version of himself or herself.

When the changes wrought by pushing the RESET button have worked their managerial magic, refocusing you on future prospects instead of current pain, it is then you will be able to consider capitalizing on what your new landscape has revealed. Downturns represent opportunity, as we all know. And "one man's trash is another's treasure" to boot. Truth be told, both of my businesses were started during (or at the tail end of) a recession. What was disaster for others became opportunity for me and my partners.

So, when you've made peace with where you are and made sure that your company is stable and profitable at whatever your revenue level has become, that's when it's time to reclaim your entrepreneurial optimism and embrace the possibilities that lie ahead.

Your Qual Card assignment for this chapter is simple and forward looking. Think of it as a hands-on training assignment, the purpose of which is to (1) learn the art of contingency planning by utilizing your COGS reports and expertise to give you a picture of your new reality and (2) show you how to move through the critical decisions as to how you will weather a crisis and with whom. The financial model you develop, combined with your overall business strategy, will be your guide moving forward. Your training will center on the budget process in the interests of getting you prepared for both the everyday storms and the major hurricanes that could buffet your business with little or no warning. It's navy-style training, the kind that leaves you better prepared to lead your organization in all sorts of weather and conditions.

Remember, just as survival is the whole game on a submarine, preserving profit and cash is what separates entrepreneurial winners from losers when hard times come. Without profit and cash, you have no business, no people, and no corporate culture to protect. So, anticipate potential trouble, use COGS to establish a plan of action that you can practice and put to use in an emergency, and if the time comes, push the RESET button to avoid your own version of the jam dive!

CHAPTER 13 QUAL CARD

Initial each requirement as met:

PREREQUISITES   INITIALS

The entrepreneur has created a "real
budget"—one that represents where he/
she really expects to be based on current
industry and macroeconomic trends—and
done all planning around this budget.   _____

The entrepreneur has created a "success
budget" for the possibility that the
company will overproduce and hit even its
stretch targets, and asked himself/herself
to consider what sorts of resources will
be required in this scenario. (This should
truly be a best-case scenario budget, not
the everyday budget of an over-optimistic
entrepreneur.)   _____

The entrepreneur has created a contingency-to-crisis budget to prepare, as the
US Navy does, for the worst-case scenario.
This budget considers potential expense
cuts to handle revenue reductions of 10,
20, 30 percent or whatever alternate
percentages the entrepreneur prefers.
Being a theoretical exercise only, showing
the entrepreneur's plan for keeping the
ship afloat in any weather, conditions, or
circumstances; this could also be termed a
"peace-of-mind" budget.   _____

The entrepreneur has created a "no-layoff" budget to war-game an attempt to keep the company profitable in a downturn without downsizing the workforce. This budget, aimed primarily at those who have taken a no-layoffs pledge, requires the entrepreneur to use a COGS analysis to identify expense-cutting options that do not affect personnel.

To complete his or her training in the area of contingency planning, crisis leadership, and the RESET button, the *Qualified* Entrepreneur has assured himself/herself that he/she is:

- ready to write the company's sequel, if need be, through the use of the RESET button;

- prepared to face consequences for making decisions that need to be made;

- well-prepared for adversity before it occurs, having scheduled contingency planning/training on an annual basis, including leadership training at various levels of the organization; and

- accepting of change—aware that it is inevitable, and confident of being able to handle it and find opportunity in it.

SIGNATURE: _____

DATE: _____

REFLECTION: PEER ADVICE AND INSIGHTS

"Though no one can go back and make a brand new start, anyone can start from now and make a brand new ending."

—CARL BARD

Life has a way of presenting us with opportunities for evaluating our actions, our achievements . . . our very lives. Every inflection point seems to cause us to reflect. In so doing, we appreciate our milestones, but we also recall the opportunities we've missed, the times we've fallen short of our own expectations, the ways we could have done things differently.

Perhaps the most significant inflection/reflection point for a business owner is the "Day of the Wire," a day I've lived out twice in my life. It's the day you cash out, sell your business, and see how well your work has paid off. It's Judgment Day without the pearly gates, because the Day of the Wire provides a final accounting of the time you've spent at the helm of your company—not in thousands of words, but in numbers that may be six to nine digits long. The sum you see wired into your bank account represents the present-day value, the goodwill, the growth, and the long-term potential you've infused into your business—and that means it can't help but be a reflection of *you*.

Imagine yourself sitting at your desk, awaiting that wire. Will your pride on the Day of the Wire outweigh your regret? Will you be pleased by the value the market has placed on your energies and efforts? Or will you be wishing you could take a mulligan on the last few years and try again?

Those of you who have experienced an exit or "liquidity event" recognize the thought pattern here. Those of you who haven't, well, perhaps it helps to think of other moments of change—a graduation, a wedding, the birth of a child, a health scare, or a significant death among friends or family. These, too, are times when we take stock. A chapter has ended; a new one is beginning. Are you happy with how things went? Are you optimistic about where things are going? Or have you made mistakes you don't care to repeat?

I have been blessed to receive feedback from my peers throughout the writing of this book, and now, as we near the end, I've asked some of my entrepreneurial friends to share some of the insights gained from the inflection/reflection points they've experienced. What have they learned in taking stock? What advice would they share? What mistakes might they want to prevent others from making? I found that their answers fell into seven broad categories, which resonate with my own experiences, too. As you read, let the words of these seasoned entrepreneurs help you take stock of your own career and life. *Take a pen and circle some key words and thoughts as you read.* The sad truth about the reflecting we do at inflection points is that the insights usually don't last—life is busy, and we often move on before putting our thoughts into action. My hope is that it'll be different for you this time and that the wise words of my peers will result in real takeaways for your leadership, your business, and your life.

BECOMING AN ENTREPRENEUR

It seems I don't know anyone who regrets starting a business:

- "I wish I had done my own thing earlier."

- "I regret not getting started earlier. Being an entrepreneur has been terrific."

- "I took the plunge later than many entrepreneurs (in my late thirties). But, looking back, I can say that nothing put my future more squarely in my own hands than the decision to strike out on my own. While it looked risky through the front window, it looks like NOT making that decision would have been even riskier in the rear-view." This commenter bucked popular opinion, too, by adding that he wished he spent more time at work!

The only additional comment I'd offer is that I think it would be helpful to most of us to really understand ourselves as we start and begin to build our businesses. It's probably like our elders telling us to relax and enjoy those very short years with our children— great advice, hard to follow. But I do think it makes for a better entrepreneurial life if you know what things make you happy in life and can build your company in ways that allow you to do them.

> But I do think it makes for a better entrepreneurial life if you know what things make you happy in life and can build your company in ways that allow you to do them.

SEEKING ADVICE AND INPUT

Hands down the most common response: "I should have networked with peers much earlier," followed by "I wish I'd found a mentor/coach/ advisory board sooner." "I think it could have saved me a lot of the basic and rookie mistakes," explained one. Wrote another, "I should have more quickly accepted that I do not know it all, and that the only way I can improve is to accept that I do not have all the answers and seek out those who are experts/those best able to help."

I agree with all of these comments. What would my partners and I have done differently in those first eight years of business had we enjoyed the sage guidance of more-experienced entrepreneurs? A *ton*. And we would have saved ourselves a lot of pain doing it.

A sampling of further thoughts:

- "It would have helped to have someone work with me to help identify and bust through limiting beliefs, because limiting beliefs are the biggest difference between entrepreneurs and the average person, as well as between successful entrepreneurs and average or unsuccessful entrepreneurs."

- "I didn't know what I didn't know—and that was a double-edged sword. I joke that I may not have started my first business if I knew all that could go wrong. But that's not true…. What I missed was hearing real-world, first-hand experience from ordinary people who had already done what I was trying to do. I think I would have proceeded more confidently, taken more risks, and grown revenues faster."

- Advice? "Look to the example of the sponge: Soak up everything you can that will help you be a better person and leader, and give back when asked. Sponges absorb, but they only release when squeezed."

You have to be willing to be vulnerable, I'd add, if you're going to benefit from peer advice. You have to let others really see you and your business if you are to get solid input from an individual or a group. One use of peer guidance that I think could be invaluable to most of us: giving our peers a copy of our vision and asking them to hold our feet to the fire until we achieve it!

PREPARING FOR BUSINESS/ACQUIRING SKILLS

Since my peers are generally happy with their careers, it's perhaps not a surprise that there aren't many regrets in this category. One respondent wishes he had taken a finance course in college or at some later point. Another says he wishes that he had finished college and maybe gone beyond it. Others recommend stretching in every direction possible:

- "Get self-awareness training early and get in the habit of asking for feedback from people all around you on 'How am I doing?'"

- "I should have taken advantage of opportunities early in my career to learn more and take on greater challenges."

My own bit of advice in this category is to apply the concept of continuous improvement not just to your company, but to yourself. This doesn't require any special effort; I just periodically ask myself what I've done lately to make me a better Randy Nelson in all categories of my life. I let the honest answers bubble up and typically they surprise me and motivate me to be better at building brand Me. If we don't take the time to make ourselves better people, it's that much more difficult to encourage others around us to become better people.

The next two categories are the beefy ones—indeed, the depth and variety of these comments were a factor in my decision to write this book. Most of us are very much aware of the things we could have done better as leaders of our companies. One of my peers succinctly described the whole scope of the struggle to become a *Qualified* Entrepreneur, saying he wishes he had been "much more intentional with the structure and strategy of my company."

STRUCTURING THE BUSINESS

The devil, as they say, is in the details:

- "I wish I would have solicited better legal advice on the setup and structure of my organization."

- "I should have had a much more formal partnership and operating agreement. People, relationships and motivations can change over time and it is better to identify as many of the rules of engagement as possible upfront in a relationship—almost like having a prenuptial agreement with your business partner."

- "I would have selected my cofounders more like life partners…which they are!"

- "I think I should have involved my wife in the financial planning for the business."

- "Put training and development systems in place for all employees."

- "I should have systematized my business and held people accountable to following the process."

- "Wish I would have put accountability systems in place earlier."

- "Should have put a three-year vision out there."

- Had he the chance to do it all again, one entrepreneur says, "I would have

Had he the chance to do it all again, one entrepreneur says, "I would have outside consultants involved, constantly asking *why we do what we do.*"

outside consultants involved, constantly asking *why we do what we do.*"

STRATEGIC LEADERSHIP

This category is a grab bag of "coulda, woulda, shoulda." But, as you'll see, there are themes in the advice—track details better, make better decisions, take a smarter approach to risk:

- "I should have done more due diligence and planning around my first business purchase."

- "By not trying to do an add-on acquisition to the engineering company, I was too conservative. We could have grown in other states."

- "I should have bought a larger business—$5–10 million in revenue. There is more momentum, more cash for professional management, and it's just as easy/hard to raise capital for that size of business as it is to raise money for a $1 million business. I think there is more untapped opportunity in the $5–10 million range."

- One wishes he had been more daring. "My mistake: not pursuing more ideas and taking them to market."

- Another commenter, however, wishes he had stuck to the knitting. "I should have focused more on being the best at our core product, not trying new things."

- One of my respondents wishes he'd "paid more attention to maintaining and nurturing client relationships."

- Meanwhile, this commenter regrets that he didn't mix it up more. "I shouldn't have let 'being nice' and avoiding conflict get in the way of good business results."

- Another thinks he knows why his Day of the Wire wasn't a happy one: "I approached my business as a 'lifestyle business' and really didn't focus directly on growing revenues or growing the value of the organization. Not being an extremely money-motivated person, I lost emotional steam once we were successful and I was able to make a market-rate salary. Employees were happy, customers were happy, cash flow was good...[So] I rested. Eventually, I seemed to lose my drive, as if I thought the challenge was over. When the timing was right to exit the business, I felt like I had less to 'show' for all the effort."

- Regrets? If this guy had a do-over, "I would have paid more attention to my market and sold when multiples were higher."

This category also brought out a lot of thoughts on the subject of new initiatives:

- "Stop talking and start doing."

- "Jump in, move quickly, and have immediate goals in mind. In the drug research business they call it a 'quick kill,' which means to get to early testing on a molecule as quickly as possible and see whether or not it is going to work before you spend the big bucks on clinical trials. I think entrepreneurship works much the same way. If there is an idea that you like, go for it. But don't fall in love with the idea; prove it by working quickly and setting goals that have to be hit. Too many bad ideas live too long. Life is too short and there are a lot of good ideas out there, so make sure you get to one."

- Agrees another: "Test small, fail quickly."

- Don't second-guess your gut: "If it doesn't feel right, it will not get better," said one of my entrepreneurial friends. "Do something about it sooner rather than later."

> Don't second-guess your gut: "If it doesn't feel right, it will not get better," said one of my entrepreneurial friends. "Do something about it sooner rather than later."

- Another faults himself for dragging his feet: "If I could do it over, I would have moved quicker on many issues that came back to bite me."

Interestingly, several of my respondents advised others to turn a skeptical eye on ideas of any kind:

- "Be objective rather than subjective in your business. Ideas may sound great, but you really don't know until you put the numbers to it and hold someone accountable."

- "You should say 'NO' to more deals than you say 'yes' to."

WORKING WITH PEOPLE

Bad hires and soft-hearted retention—that's the story in this category. Regrets?

- "Not investing in top talent."

- "Cheaping out," another commenter agrees. "When we were trying to get out of my company, we decided to hire a person to run the business so that we could move onto our other businesses. Ultimately, we chose to hire someone who didn't have all of the qualifications we wanted because they weren't that expensive. Horrible decision. The experts always say to hire someone that you think is better or smarter than you are. Unfortunately, we didn't listen to that advice. The business went sideways for a year, and we ultimately had to sell it."

- "Not being quicker to let folks go who were not a good fit for their position."

- "Hoping the 'C' player will get better. They don't. We just hope, teach, and tolerate them. Hope, by definition, is not a strategy that implies that we have any control. By 'tolerating,' we send a strong message about ourselves and our organization to all employees, customers, and vendors. Think of it this way: in an athletic event, we look to take advantage of an opponent's weak spot. There is no good reason to allow our 'weak spots' to make our businesses vulnerable to defeat."

- "Not making decisions based on what's best for the business instead of [what's best for] the employee."

COULDA'S AND SHOULDA'S?

- "Employ smart, experienced advisers and team [members] and then ask them for help. Stop thinking it's heroic to do it all [by yourself]."

- "I should have hired a #2 person sooner. Once I hired him, my business boomed."

- "If I had it to do over, I would have spent more time doing due diligence on key hires. We made several mistakes. When you're growing fast you want to make quick decisions, but some decisions you should take time with, and be very mindful of the importance of the decision."

- "Select a great team and then get them focused on something specific."

- Another commenter agrees, and takes it a step further: "Surround yourself with smart, successful, and motivated people . . . both *inside and outside* of your business."

- "Create a culture where your employees are valued and their feedback is encouraged. Attracting and retaining top talent will create success, regardless of what business you are in."

- One commenter offers his opinion that hiring "experienced" salesmen "is way overrated." He explains why: "They often come in feeling they know how to do things, and want to tell you and the prospects how much they know. Plus, half of the 'experienced' salesmen are not real salesmen. They are only experienced at visiting, talking and driving around." Granted, he says, some sales jobs require particular technical knowledge. "But 90 percent of us should be looking for those with the right DNA, and then training them in the necessary product knowledge." His current definition of a hot prospect for sales excellence? "Former athlete who hates to lose and knows how to win. Problem solver. Knows how to ask questions and LISTEN to the answers. And it wouldn't hurt if [his or her] father was a salesman, too."

- "Act quickly once you have made a hiring mistake. There were many times that I knew I should let someone go for performance or because it just wasn't working out, but almost always I took too long to act."

- "Measure progress toward annual goals weekly—for the company, departments, and even to the individual level. For example, if the order entry department has four people, do you think they all perform the same? Measure the number of orders and [the monetary value] of the orders each day, and the cream will rise to the top." Don't be queasy about identifying who's merit-worthy and who's not, he adds: "The high achievers will have more job satisfaction because of the recognition, and the deadwood will resign."

MAINTAINING A FAMILY/PERSONAL LIFE

I've long been envious of two of my friends, both air-traffic controllers. When they're home or on the golf course, they're fully present in the relaxation of the moment. And why shouldn't they be? There are no planes to land at home or on the golf course!

But that's not how entrepreneurs live, because being an entrepreneur is more than a full-time challenge. When I was in the thick of it in my fast-growth years, the days (hours?) when I didn't think about the business were few and far between. There was good reason for this: if I let the business fail, I would be risking the livelihoods of my employees, not to mention my own financial security and my family's. For me, the worst times were the holidays in the years that the business was struggling. Oh, how I wanted to just kick back and relax, enjoying time with family and friends! But, in the back of my mind, I was running numbers, devising strategies, thinking about what I could do when I got back to work.

Detaching from the office and its concerns is a worthy goal, but for most entrepreneurs, it's all but impossible. We think about the business because we have to. Businesses can't be put on hold. You have to always be processing the past, dealing with the present, and planning for the future—because that's the burden we carry when we elect to start and run a company. But we also think about business in our off-hours because we *want* to. It's sport to us, a mission and calling, and yes, even recreation. Realistically speaking, home and family are only going to get a percentage of our attention, and the best we can do as spouses and parents is to try continually to increase the percentage.

Being an entrepreneur with a family necessarily involves trade-offs. There are choices, and there are costs. If you're truly driven, the days you spend working late or traveling impose a cost on both you and your family. If you've taken a stand in favor of operating more of a lifestyle business, which is a valid choice, you have to be aware that your availability for family activities, while great, imposes a ceiling on your company's potential. My advice: *know which side of the fence you're on and accept the consequences.* Don't beat yourself up for failing to build a stellar company if you're running a lifestyle business and nurturing a family. And don't disparage the cost on your free time if you're addicted to the growth drug or trying to protect your employees' livelihoods during a time of economic downturn or business setback.

I haven't been a perfect husband or parent, but I'm proud of what I have been able to accomplish to date. I built two businesses (with a third in the building stage), and wrote a book. All along the way, I was as engaged as I possibly could be in family life as Kristi and I raised our six kids together to adulthood and welcomed four grandsons, as of this writing. My wife and I agree that our kids greatly benefited from my presence and passionate interest in them. My thoughts were often elsewhere, but the kids never knew that, so they didn't feel cheated by my inability to leave the business at the office. My wife, of course, always knew whenever I wasn't fully present, but she understood that being fully present isn't really possible for an entrepreneur. What worked for us was to stay in close and open communication, as husband and wife, and continually plan or adjust to provide the best family experience possible for all of us. I am a lucky man, for Kristi has made it clear many times over the years that I always do the best I can, and that she knows it.

The burdens of starting and running a business are many, and they don't go away. But nothing I've said should be construed to mean that I don't think we should be working to lay those burdens down when we can. As much as our families need participation from us, *we need it for ourselves and our sanity*—and I wish you luck in finding real leisure in your life. In the building phase of my career, I found I never really could "get away" unless I was on extended vacation—and preferably away from phones and computers. I wish that had been different for me, and I think I'm doing better at finding respite as I get older. But young'uns, please: look at the comments from your elders (me and my peers), and try to do better than we have:

- "Pay as much attention to your personal life and relationships as you pay to your work and career. Balance is important."

- "I wish I would have paid more attention to my wife and marriage, and not made assumptions or taken things for granted."

- "I regret not being a better husband, and believing what my father told me about women being irrational. I've since learned that if someone in my life appears to be acting irrationally, I either don't understand their point of view or don't have enough information."

- "Remember that if you're married, it's her business too. You need to manage her 'investment' as much or more than you would an economic investor's or a bank's."

- "I regret not taking more time to step back [from the business]. In the early days I worked too much and burned myself out and missed opportunities in my personal life. You will never look back and say 'I wish I spent more time working,' but you will almost certainly look back and say, 'I wish I had spent more time with family, friends, or doing things I like.'"

I'll give myself the last word on this section. When my grandfather was about 90 years old I asked him what made the biggest difference in his life, what was most important to him. He was very clear: family. He didn't mention working hard, saving money, or having a comfortable retirement—all of which he had done. His family, he said, was the cornerstone of his life.

That being said, I think we all deserve to add ourselves to the priority list. In years past, I often said, "I have no life outside of business and family." I'm striving to do things differently now—and so are many of my entrepreneurial colleagues.

I have three bits of advice for all of us, including me. First, I think we entrepreneurs should figure out what activities renew our

> I think we entrepreneurs should figure out what activities renew our spirit for us, reevaluate frequently, and find ways of doing more of whatever's currently on the list.

spirit for us, reevaluate frequently, and find ways of doing more of whatever's currently on the list. Second, and related to the first, I think we should each keep trying to enlarge our focus beyond the everyday challenges of entrepreneurial business—we miss a lot when we always keep our heads down! The last piece of advice is something I'll pass along from Bronnie Ware, palliative care nurse and author of *The Top Five Regrets of the Dying: A Life Transformed by the Dearly Departing.*[1] She lists what people most often say on their deathbed:

1. I wish I had the courage to live a life true to myself, not the life others expected of me.

2. I wish I hadn't worked so hard.

3. I wish I had the courage to express my feelings.

4. I wish I had stayed in touch with friends.

5. I wish I had let myself be happier.

How many of these dying wishes can you remove from the list before you reach *your* final days?

CHAPTER 14 QUAL CARD

Initial each requirement as met.

PREREQUISITES

INITIALS

The entrepreneur has imagined the "Day of the Wire" and spent time taking stock of how he/she is likely to feel at such a major career inflection point. This includes considering what the company's value may be, what structural and strategic decisions have contributed to its valuation, and how leading their company has affected the entrepreneur's family/personal life.

_____

Using advice from experienced entrepreneurs circled above, the entrepreneur has identified any changes he/she may wish to make—either inside the company or to his/her life balance—before reaching the Day of the Wire.

_____

In preparation for filling out a final assessment of all Qual Cards within this book, the entrepreneur has established whether he/she is leading a growth company or a lifestyle business and whether the type identified matches the entrepreneur's own life and career goals.

_____

SIGNATURE: _____

DATE: _____

CHAPTER 15

THE SECOND DECISION

"The truth of the matter is that you always know the right thing to do, the hard part is doing it."

—GENERAL H. NORMAN SCHWARZKOPF

Your life's journey continues, but your self-awareness journey—as guided by this book—is reaching an end. With the outline of the requirements of the Entrepreneur Qual Card (Appendix B) now complete, there's only one thing left for you to do: **Make the Second Decision.**

I am using this final chapter to invite you to commit, today and forever, to becoming a *Qualified* Entrepreneur. To do so is to join a movement to enhance entrepreneurial success and decrease the rate of entrepreneurial failure, for the benefit of the world we all live in. As I've told you, the business failure statistic—70 percent of entrepreneurial businesses are gone within 10 years and 50 percent don't make it even 5 years—bothers me a great deal. As I've also said, 24 years of starting and running businesses alongside peers doing the same has shown me that we entrepreneurs are part of the problem—and that we should become the solution.

To make this change, you also need to understand that the Entre-preneur Qual Card is just the beginning. There is significantly more for you to learn in the future as a lifelong learner; areas such as management and leadership, and sales and marketing, are obviously on the list and there are countless others!

My intent was to raise your self-awareness around your own strengths, weaknesses, capabilities and limitations. "Only about five in 1000 people have the aptitude for starting and growing a big business. In comparison, 20 in 1000 have IQ's high enough to be accepted into Mensa."[1]

There are few, if any, good statistics that illustrate to what extent post-startup entrepreneurs underperform in their businesses, but my guess is that it's potentially significant. John Mullins, PhD, noted author and associate professor of management practice at London Business School recently stated (at a seminar I heard him speak at in 2014): "Most Mid-Market companies grow slower than they should". I am a strong believer that accountability starts at the top, and that businesses are a long-lasting reflection of their founders' strengths and weaknesses. So, as you end your journey in this book and sit down to make your Second Decision as to what comes next, here is my request:

Hold yourself accountable first. Prior to asking your direct reports and employees to hold themselves accountable, give them your commitment to becoming a *Qualified* Entrepreneur first.

If there is anything in the boxed paragraph above that gives you qualms, take note. It may be an early indicator of the ultimate choice you'll make in this chapter—the Second Decision choice of whether to **lead**, **support**, or **create** in the next phase of your entrepreneurial career.

So let's recap, shall we? **And, remember: you caused the problem, not me!** You're the one that built a successful company, one that has survived the initial startup phase! As you read, fill in the blanks so that you have a reference to review prior to your final Qual Card decision.

SECTION A: In Chapter 2, I identified four issues that prevent entrepreneurs from becoming *Qualified* Entrepreneurs *(check all that apply to you)*:

____ Insistence on autonomy

____ Unwillingness to build structure, cultivate expertise, or delegate responsibility

____ Boredom

____ Failure to engage in self-examination

SECTION B: Review the definition of the *Disciplined* Entrepreneur (your first step towards becoming a *Qualified* Entrepreneur) and check all that apply to you:

The *Disciplined* Entrepreneur is one who:

_____ becomes fully self-aware that *they don't know what they don't know*, and that it's better to achieve a status of *"I know what I don't know."* This self-knowledge makes it clear how the entrepreneur's shortcomings may be affecting his or her company . . . and usually results in a commitment to a lifelong learning process.

_____ becomes fully self-aware that for the business to succeed long term, a transition must occur from the business being about "me" as its entrepreneur/CEO to being about the overall needs of the company.

_____ commits to undertaking the preparation necessary for making the Second Decision. This is a conscious choice to acquire a more disciplined approach to management and leadership—or to bring that discipline to the company in another way. The *Disciplined* Entrepreneur knows that it's less important how his or her role is shaped than that the company excels and succeeds.

SECTION C. Review the top reasons why small businesses fail (I am taking a very educated guess that the same issues below also relate directly to underperformance for any size organization).[2, 3, 4] (*Check all that apply to your current organization.*)

Ironically during two of my career's highest public moments (Entrepreneur of the Year (EOY) ceremony where I was a finalist for the Carolinas Region EOY award (2001) and during the Inc. 500 awards banquet in 2007 (NSTAR was #163) – I was dealing internally with the reality that Orion and NSTAR respectively were in the middle of their most challenging (and potentially life threatening) time periods in their corporate lives. Success can be very fleeting if we are not careful!

___ The math just doesn't work – There's not enough demand for your product or service at a price that will produce a profit.

___ CEOs who cannot get out of their own way – Whether they express it by avoiding conflict or risk, or by displaying perfectionist, paranoid, self-righteous, or greedy tendencies—and sometimes all of them at once—stubbornness is the identifying characteristic of many entrepreneurs who are destined to fail. Even after the problems have been repeatedly pointed out by others and even acknowledged by the CEO himself/herself, these CEOs continue making the same mistakes.

___ Out-of-control growth – This would include over-expansion, moving into markets that are less profitable, experiencing growing pains that damage the business, or borrowing too much money in an attempt to keep growth at a particular rate. Sometimes less is more!

___ Poor accounting – You cannot be in control of your business if you don't know what is really going on in it, financially speaking.

___ Lack of a cash cushion – As we said in Chapter 7, six months' cash (and covenants) is king!

___ Operational mediocrity – Often the problem is being unwilling or unable to terminate non-performers and get the right people in the right seats.

____ Operational inefficiencies – Many struggling companies haven't figured out how to manage or control expenses, which depresses profits.

____ Dysfunctional management – Not enough focus, vision, planning, standards, and other requirements of good management.

____ The lack of a succession plan – Statistics show that only 35 percent of family businesses survive past the first generation of ownership and only 20 percent survive to a third generation. If anything, the statistics are worse in nonfamily businesses. Part of the problem: owners see succession as an event instead of a process.

____ A declining market – A bad economy or structural changes in an industry will always reveal managerial skill—or lack of it.

SECTION D: Compile and review your QE Notebook

After gathering data from my peers and gaining additional insight into what each of you reviews on a routine basis (daily/weekly/ monthly), I have listed below what ought to be included in a complete QE Notebook, at least for the majority of you. (Some companies or industries may require more or fewer documents.)

- Income statement

- Balance sheet

- Cash-flow statement

- Daily cash reports

- Budget reports—actual vs. budget expenditures

- Sales/forecast/key performance indicators/dashboards—customized to your business

- Accounting reports (AR/AP)

- Customer satisfaction data

- Customized reports for your business

Throughout the book, I have asked you to add more documents to your QE Notebook. These are listed below, with the pertinent chapters in parentheses. Check each one that is already in your notebook as CEO of the company.

____ Your stock certificate (Chapter 2)

____ Your PRF personality profile results (Chapter 4)

____ Your CEO performance rating chart (Chapter 5)

____ Your analysis of the three to five major changes a replacement CEO would make (Chapter 5)

____ Your completed *One-Page Strategic Plan* (Chapter 6)

____ A copy of your personal guarantees with the bank (Chapter 7)

____ Your six months' cash report of cash flow (Chapter 7)

____ Your six months' covenants forecast (Chapter 7)

____ Your three-year COGS report (Chapter 8)

____ Your three-year metrics (Chapter 9)

____ Your payroll COGS report (Chapter 9)

____ Your combined timelines (Chapter 15)

The QE Notebook paints a truthful picture for you, because all of the items in it come from an objective base. I want you to have your own company's data with you when you make your critical decisions. You need your baseline financials and your analysis of them. These, combined with your intuition as an entrepreneur, will lead to more disciplined and informed decisions.

> **Whether you like the picture painted by your QE Notebook or not, it is the truth, and a *Qualified* Entrepreneur must be grounded in the truth of his or her business.**

Whether you like the picture painted by your QE Notebook or not, it is the truth, and a *Qualified* Entrepreneur must be grounded in the truth of his or her business. You are accustomed to looking at what profit you make and your sales levels. Most of you focus on whether you have cash today, too. The *Qualified* Entrepreneur wants more—in fact, he or she wants to know the truth of every item or measurement we've discussed throughout this book and wants to have it at his or her fingertips when decisions need to be made. Cash trends are critical. Your stock price indicates the market value you have built into the business. Metrics reveal productivity and its trends. Personal guarantees are real and must be remembered. COGS is gold waiting to be mined…and the list goes on.

SECTION E: Review Your Leadership Options as a Qualified Entrepreneur *(After reviewing and considering the options, mark the role you are choosing.)*

___ **The Leader.**

> This could be the founder, the owner/operator—the captain of the ship, if you will. Regardless of title, this is the *Qualified* Entrepreneur who, at any stage of the company's growth, wants to self-qualify as CEO. He or she has the capabilities and is willing to commit to the work and learning necessary to lead the company, as well to put the right people in the right seats to support a vision. In this choice, the *Qualified* Entrepreneur, and/or the executive team, is charged with instilling discipline throughout the organization as well as making their own consistent and disciplined leadership decisions.

___ **The Role Player.**

> This *Qualified* Entrepreneur prefers not to be CEO at all, or wishes to leave that role after a certain point in the growth cycle. The Role Player is willing to hire the right people to operate the company so that he or she can pursue passions inside the company. Alternate roles for the entrepreneur in this choice could include chairman, board member, inventor, chief sales officer, and COO, to name a few.

___ **The Creator.**

This *Qualified* Entrepreneur loves the company that he or she has built, but doesn't want to be the CEO. The Creator prefers to hire the right people to operate the business, so that he or she can be free to pursue passions outside the company. Entrepreneurs who itch to start multiple companies are the perfect fit here. In addition, this could be the path for a CEO who is ready to retire or turn the business over to a new CEO and move on to some non-entrepreneurial pursuit. In all cases, the Creator understands that it is critically important to leave behind a disciplined company, and that the highest expression of this type is to "pay it forward" as a *Qualified* Entrepreneur who brings the same structure and commitment to his or her new venture.

SECTION F: Review your Timelines

As you can see, I have inserted my combined timelines below and left space for you to do the same.

COMBINED BUSINESS & EDUCATION TIMELINE/LIFELINE

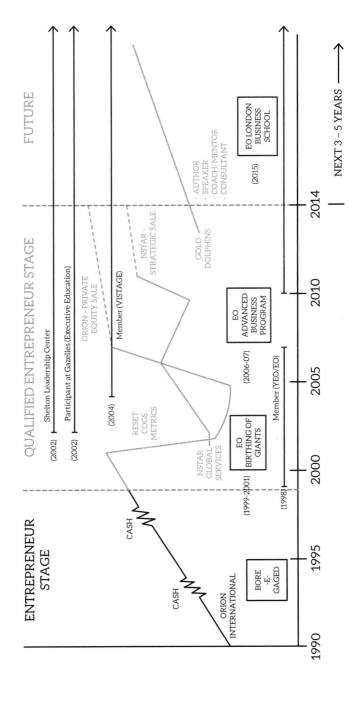

COMBINED BUSINESS & EDUCATION TIMELINE/LIFELINE

NEXT 3 – 5 YEARS ⟶

In making your Second Decision to become a *Qualified* Entrepreneur, the critical part of the timeline to pay attention to is the right-hand side, where it shows your estimation of the trend line over the next three to five years. More specifically:

- Are you expanding your business by leaps and bounds *and* starting a family or dealing with other major changes in your life activities? If so, how will you be both places at once? Are you set up for success in both?

- Are you hitting a growth streak at a time when your health is suffering, or the difficulties of aging are catching up with you?

- Does the graph for the next three to five years excite you or depress you? For example, have you just come through a very difficult period, only to find yourself staring straight at another mountain to climb, just to keep your company on its feet?

- Is there anything else on your combined timeline that leaves you saying, "Uh-oh, this could be a problem"? (i.e., where are you set up for failure or conflict?)

- Looking to the left, to the part of your combined timeline that reflects the past, what parts do you want to replicate in your future? What parts do you want to make sure never happen again?

It's inevitable that life will get in the way of business and vice-versa; it really can't be prevented. This exercise is intended as a thinking and planning tool. You can and should use your Timeline/Lifeline to take note of potential trouble spots, and discuss them with a spouse or business partner, your CEO peers, your coach, or your board of directors/advisers. If you lack some or all of these sources of input, well, let this be another indicator of a situation to be remedied. Appendix A will also be very helpful to you as you ponder these questions above as it adds the personal/family timelines for your overall review.

> You can and should use your Timeline/ Lifeline to take note of potential trouble spots, and discuss them with a spouse or business partner, your CEO peers, your coach, or your board of directors/ advisers.

I have left you a blank timeline; this is to allow you to draw the graph of how your industry is trending against a corresponding graph of the overall economy. Where in the cycle is your industry—trending up, trending down, or suffering disruption? How do these trend lines affect the issues you've identified in your other graphs? What effect might these trend lines have on the Second Decision you're about to make?

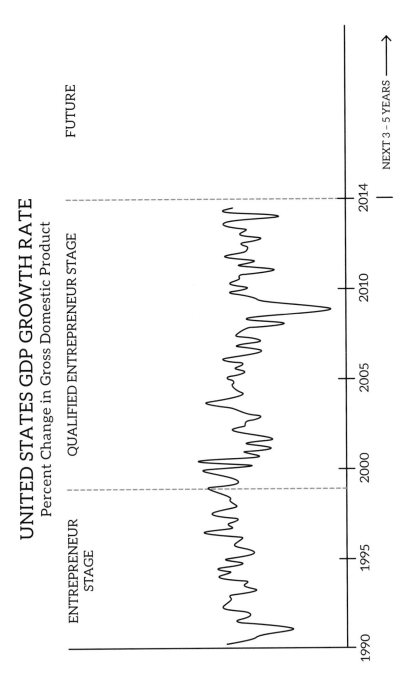

THE SECOND DECISION

UNITED STATES GDP GROWTH RATE
Percent Change in Gross Domestic Product

ENTREPRENEUR
STAGE

QUALIFIED ENTREPRENEUR STAGE

FUTURE

1990   1995   2000   2005   2010   2014

NEXT 3 – 5 YEARS ⟶

261

YOUR INDUSTRY & ECONOMY TIMELINE/LIFELINE

NEXT 3 – 5 YEARS ⟶

THE SECOND DECISION: CHOOSING YOUR ROLE

Congratulations on making it this far! It's been quite a journey, and it's been my pleasure to have joined you on it! Now comes the most important part: After all of your reading, thinking, analyzing, and planning, what are you going to commit to? In which role will you commit to doubling your personal capacity in the next three years?[5]

My good friend, Rear Admiral (Ret.) Benny Suggs believes—and passionately states—that **"callings trump careers."** Having served 30 years in the US Navy (deputy commander in chief for US Special Operations Command, and captain of the USS *America*, CV-66), as well as a very successful stint at Harley-Davidson, he is currently executive director of the NC State Alumni Association, and he has caused many a business executive to stop and really consider the meaning of the phrase. What *is* my calling? What is yours?

My calling is to be a *Qualified* Entrepreneur (I have spent significant time in all three roles over the past 25 years:s Leader, Role Player, and Creator). I love to create and lead businesses that are sustainable and market leading, but there's more to it than that: **I firmly believe in eventually turning my companies over to great leaders, to give them an opportunity to make my companies better, so that I**

> I also have the firm belief that there comes a point for all of us when we are not the best person to lead the organization into the future.

can go out and create again. That is my calling. I also have the firm belief that there comes a point for all of us when we are not the best person to lead the organization into the future. And what's crucial for each of us is to determine when that's the case, instead of letting others decide the timing for us.

Think about whether you are continuing to build your legacy, or starting to taint it.

Since my departures from Orion and NSTAR, new leaders have taken the reins and propelled the companies to greater heights— and this is as it should be. **They were the right people at the right time with the right skill set to lead these organizations into the future.** I am forever grateful to them for this, so thanks Bill, Mike, Tim, L.J., and Darrell!

I can honestly say that when I left Orion and NSTAR, my Entrepreneur Qual Card was complete. Here's a quote that resonates for me from a recent Gazelles Educational Summit:

> *"The measure of a leader is what happens when you are gone. The leader embeds his greatness in his people and in his processes."*
>
> —Captain David Marqet, author: *Turn The Ship Around*

I am proud but humbled to know that I left both Orion and NSTAR as disciplined organizations ready to thrive under the direction of their next leaders, and that both companies have continued to excel for their customers and employees. I will always savor that moment when both companies were on the Fast

50 list, nos. 8 and 9, after 20-plus and 10-plus years in business, respectively. As the commercial says . . . *priceless*.

As we drive now toward your final commitment and Second Decision, I have inserted the highlights from a letter I asked my Vistage Coach ("Master Chair" Bill Buxton) to write to the entrepreneurs reading this book:

Dear prospective *Qualified* Entrepreneur:

I have been coaching and advising owners and CEOs of small to midsized businesses for the last 35 years. One of the most painful situations I observe is what I might call the case of the "misplaced CEO." These people usually own the company they lead or at least have the majority power over it. They are almost always extremely smart and caring people and unusually gifted in one or more areas of their company's dealings. However, they are not well suited to be the head person. They are noticeably weak in one or more key areas: strategizing, leading, visioning, controlling costs, managing people, juggling priorities, delegating, organizing, evaluating risks, staying on task, etc. Many of them are keen to get "the right people in the right seats on the bus," but lose their courage or objectivity when looking at themselves. Most of them know in their hearts that they are not performing that well in their current role, but pride or prestige or fear or misplaced loyalties prevent them from stepping away. Frankly, in many cases they seem to think that the owner of a smaller enterprise *has* to be the CEO.

There is a great cost as a result of these leaders working from misplaced positions. Their companies are not performing well. Their profit margins and growth rates are well below what they should—and can—be. Their employees are unhappy and disgruntled, even if they may not feel free to say so. The leaders themselves are unfulfilled and often feel like imposters. They are not doing what they love during the work day, so this takes its toll on their stress level and on their level of satisfaction and fulfillment. All of this, of course, will take a toll on the leader's family and health, if not already, then sooner or later.

I encourage you to use this Qual Card very objectively, which may mean letting others help you assess the answers. When Randy asks you if you are *committed* to developing the skills and practices to be a *Qualified* Entrepreneur, be sure you know what he means by "commitment." Far too often I observe that for many people commitment means "I know I should" or "I really want to" or "I'm going to really try." That's not what he means and that's not what will get the job done. Don't say you're committed unless you're prepared to do whatever it takes to get there; to put other priorities on the back burner, if necessary; to create your development plan and stick to it.

Let's revisit the qualifiers and half-answers all too often heard when Mr. Buxton asks a CEO to step up to the next level of leadership, that of *Qualified* Entrepreneur:

"I know I should."

"I really want to."

"I'm going to really try."

As you grapple with your own level of commitment, let me suggest some questions for you to ponder. Write down your answers:

What do I have to do (the company needs me to do this) to grow the business over the next three years?

_____

_____

_____

What would I love to do to in my business over the next three years?

_____

_____

_____

If I could wake up tomorrow and *script my perfect day in my work life*, what would it look like, and why?

_____

_____

_____

What does success look like in my life in the next three years?

_____

_____

_____

After allowing you to spend some quality time off to attend to your self-awareness and leadership journey, I have the following question for you:

Are you the right person to lead your organization for the next three years? Or is there someone better than you, taking into account both your own needs and desires and the needs and desires of the company?

Here are your three *Qualified* Entrepreneur choices.

1. **"Yes, I am the right person."** You have the desire to lead, it fits well with your career goals and personal life, and you are prepared to commit to becoming a *Qualified* Entrepreneur. This is the Leader choice and it means you will stay CEO or president.

2. **"No, I am not the right person, but I desire to remain in the organization."** This is a choice to switch to a role of support. You are prepared to commit to becoming a *Qualified* Entrepreneur and to hire your replacement and ensure that they become a *Qualified* Entrepreneur. This is the Role Player choice, and the next part of the conversation will be regarding what sort of role you wish to play.

3. **"No, I am not the right person, and I wish to leave the organization.** You are choosing to be a Creator— either in the manner of a serial entrepreneur who seeks new opportunities to start businesses or in some other fashion that may or may not be part of the business world. If you know you want to continue creating and that you are not the right person to lead the organization

at this stage of its growth, your first responsibility as a *Qualified* Entrepreneur is to assist the organization in finding your replacement, ensuring that they commit to becoming a *Qualified* Entrepreneur.

When I completed all my US Navy Qual Cards and check-outs and finally received my captain's approval to drive the submarine, I was full of pride. But I was also very aware of the responsibility the achievement carried. From then on, my day-to-day actions and decisions affected not just me, but the entire ship and its crew. It's the same for you. Your leadership decisions as CEO carry the same heft, scope, and consequences. *Your employees ultimately need to be led by someone who is functioning at their highest and best level.* What they want and need is a *Qualified* Entrepreneur, who has committed to the role of the Leader.

I leave you with these last thoughts:

I have given you the basics, the required knowledge levels to become a *Qualified* Entrepreneur. I have tried my best to focus on elements of your job that will still be required in 3, 5, even 15 years from now; those elements are the most damaging to the organization when not done well, ultimately leading to either underperformance or, worst

Your employees ultimately need to be led by someone who is functioning at their highest and best level. What they want and need is a Qualified Entrepreneur, who has committed to the role of the Leader.

case, failure. The basics of running a business should remain the same forever, similar to your company's core values. Other areas of your business change dramatically over time (such as the development of social networking), which is why I have encouraged you in this book to *engage in lifelong learning so you can remain qualified with the ability to lead, support, or create as our entrepreneurial workspace continues its rapid evolution.* (How much change have Facebook, Google, Skype, and LinkedIn alone brought about in the past decade?)

So: be your best version of yourself, stay disciplined, and in the process, show your company how to be the best version of itself too. **What you look and act like on the outside is your brilliance, but the discipline you consistently display to yourself on the inside will become your true differentiator.**

The Entrepreneur Qual Card is in Appendix B. I invite you to read Appendix C which reveals the answer to the seawater question, as well as Appendix A to read an excerpt from the next book in my Decision Series for Entrepreneurs: *The Third Decision*. While *The Second Decision* was all about business and becoming a *Qualified* Entrepreneur, *The Third Decision* will be about your battle as a *Qualified* Entrepreneur, to live and lead a balanced life.

An Excerpt from *The Third Decision*

CHECKING THE BLOCKS

Growing a business takes a lot of time and plenty of focus. It's far too easy to overlook the importance of the rest of your life, that is until someone grabs you by the scruff of the neck and demands your attention. Here's how it usually goes for successful entrepreneurs. You start a company. It takes off. You hire, grow, and hire some more. A management structure develops with you at the top of it. Your people make good money and get promoted. What else is there to do but grow some more? Now your company is growing its revenues and profits each year and the local and regional accolades are rolling in. And new businesses are being created as well.

By now, you have read *The Second Decision* and have decided on your role for the next three to five years as a *Qualified* Entrepreneur. Congratulations! Whether you are leading, assisting, or creating, it's exciting to know that your organization is achieving its maximum potential. We're talking momentum, on every scale you choose to measure! Opening new offices, starting a new company, focusing on your new role in your expanding business—

it's exhilarating. You have just finished off another passionate day at work, singing quite loudly to your favorite song on the radio on your way home...

And...boom! You get home late, exhausted but also glowing with satisfaction, only to encounter a spouse/partner (and kids, for you parents out there) that are far less enthusiastic about the day. Maybe the little ones were difficult, or school was frustrating for the big ones, or the dog won't quit barking, or the water heater is on the fritz. And in you come, talking about your latest skirmishes on the entrepreneurial battlefield—the new market you will enter, the networking you'll do at an out-of-town conference, and the big presentation you need to prepare.

Suddenly everybody's day gets worse. Your spouse/partner doesn't share your excitement over things that will only take you away from home for more hours of the day. Your kids don't want to hear that Dad will miss the soccer game or the school play. Not surprisingly, your feelings are hurt. You wonder why the family doesn't understand what you're doing for them by building this business. It irritates you that they don't appreciate it.

> From that perspective, it's often hard to recognize that what's good news to us is often bad news to the people we care about most.

I know all too well that the one at fault here might just be you. Why? It's quite possibly that the Big Cheese at work has lost contact with what is happening (or not happening) at home. As entrepreneurs, we too often let our focus narrow to a point that all we can really see is the business. From that perspective, it's often hard to recognize that what's good news to us is often bad news to the people we care about most. New market? Out-of-town conference? Big presentation? Your spouse's/partner's reaction is bound to be sarcastic. "Fantastic, now I get to see you even less and do even more by myself here at home!"

I'm certainly guilty of it. My wife and I have raised six children together over the past 19 years, and I've spent 30 years as the businessman coming home to a family that wanted more from me. Not more money, but more of the other stuff: more time, more help, more recognition of what it takes to run a household…more me. Really, the role of an entrepreneurial spouse is similar to the role a military spouse plays. Each requires that the spouse be an independent person who can thrive in the absence of the wife or husband who is training or fighting…or building a company. An entrepreneur isn't physically gone, for the most part, but mentally? You bet. Even when we are home and supposedly "there," we never quite find the business brain off switch. If we're not careful, we leave our spouses feeling abandoned and lonely.

Question: When you started your business and began envisioning its path to success, did those future goggles focus on your personal life and the people in it? Did you spend any time thinking about how they would fit into your plans?

If you were like me, you didn't. You just became a workaholic on all fronts. By staying scrupulously organized, you managed to accomplish the amazing feat of both nurturing the business and showing up for your spouse/partner/parent role. I always made time for the kids' concerts and sports contests, and I truly loved that part of my life—especially the years of baseball coaching when my two boys were young. I thought I was setting a pretty high bar for myself—excellence, both personally and professionally—and clearing it pretty easily. Then, one day, I walked through the front door at home after a full day of work and an evening of coaching. After I'd settled into a chair on the porch with a cold drink and a satisfied sigh, I congratulated myself for not having missed the game. Good dad!

Now, you should know that my wife, Kristi, is not at all reluctant to share what she thinks, and I respect her greatly for it. I also know that I would not have been nearly as successful in my business career if she had not been equally successful leading our home and raising our kids, I am blessed to have been on her team for the past 19 years because at home she is the CEO! She was extremely appreciative of my commitment to our family as well, and always able to see the big picture of my life, never wanting me to be sorry later for missed opportunities at home.

In the early days of building my company, Kristi asked me, bluntly, "Do you even know what you're doing?" Well, I could tell from the look on her face, that night on the porch, that she was about to do it again. This time the question was equally blunt and similarly designed to force me to face the truth. "But were you here—really all the way here? Are you here now?" It was her belief that I was only hitting my marks, as an actor would on a stage, or checking off the blocks on some sort of master list of responsibilities.

When you're checking the blocks, you accomplish everything you set out to, but the measurement is strictly one of quantity— and more is always better. If I'm checking a lot of blocks, I'm winning, right? But my wife's measurements have always been a bit different, involving quality. Her point: Yes, I was fantastic at getting to everything each day, week, month…but was I really there…all the way there? Whoa. Talk about bursting my bubble.

She wasn't wrong. I didn't see it immediately, of course, but when I was able to really think about it, she had a point. I was often distracted. I took after-hours phone calls. I scribbled notes to myself on napkins. And let's just say that engaging in family events wasn't always pure joy, and sometimes it was missing entirely. I was there, doing everything I was supposed to do, but was I really "in the moment" with my family? Or was I just checking the blocks? Dinner, check. Baseball game, check. Until my wife confronted me, I was basically phoning in everything having to do with family life, I thought I was doing what I was supposed to do. That's because I really didn't know that there was any way other than checking the blocks.

I've come to see that growth is great for businesses, but it almost demands contractions in family life, a reduction of your true presence at home. The more the company requires of us during working hours, the more hollowed-out entrepreneurs can become after five o'clock. What's weird, though, is that it doesn't work the same way for our spouses/partners. They ride the rollercoaster with us much more than we sometimes realize. Whoever waits at home feels the twists, turns, climbs, and drops in our entrepreneurial career almost as intensely as we do. They take the brunt of it when we come home battered and ready to vent, and the energy they spend bucking us up again after a defeat is considerable. Even in times that are good for business, times of great entrepreneurial success, a wife or partner is on full alert, whether we want them to be or not, watching for the first signs of trouble. It's exhausting. Kristi has told me that, as much as she wanted to be part of my struggles, there were times when the kids were young and very demanding that it was actually a relief to see me and my negative energy depart for a few days on the road.

Does this sound uncomfortably familiar to you? The temptation is strong, of course, to dismiss the harm that's being done to your family life by your entrepreneurial drive. "It's just this phase," you'll tell yourself—and I know, because I've said exactly that. Or, "It's not that bad; the family seems to be fine." You could be right. But, suppose you're wrong? *If you could look into a crystal ball and see a future of damaged relationships, missed opportunities, and too many milestones that you only experienced second-hand—would you still commit wholeheartedly to growing your company at the exclusion of everything else?*

That's all I'm asking of you in this chapter—to take a clear-eyed look at what's really happening in your key relationships. Think about what you're doing and to what end, and then, to avoid regrets later, consider whether you need to make a stronger commitment to a more balanced life.

What was my "Aha" after reviewing my personal lifeline I ask you to complete below? The peak of my family activities with my kids came at the same point in time as the most difficult period in my business...I had to be two places at once and neither were willing to give...What is your "Aha"?

FAMILY/PERSONAL TIMELINE/LIFELINE

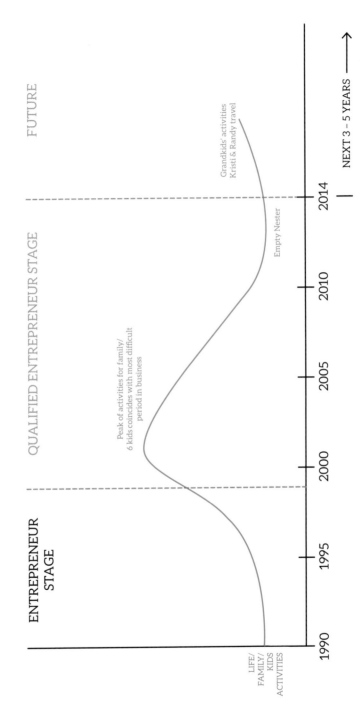

ENTREPRENEUR STAGE

QUALIFIED ENTREPRENEUR STAGE

FUTURE

LIFE/FAMILY/KIDS ACTIVITIES

Peak of activities for family/6 kids coincides with most difficult period in business

Empty Nester

Grandkids' activities
Kristi & Randy travel

1990   1995   2000   2005   2010   2014

NEXT 3 – 5 YEARS →

COMBINED BUSINESS, EDUCATION, & FAMILY/PERSONAL TIMELINE/LIFELINE

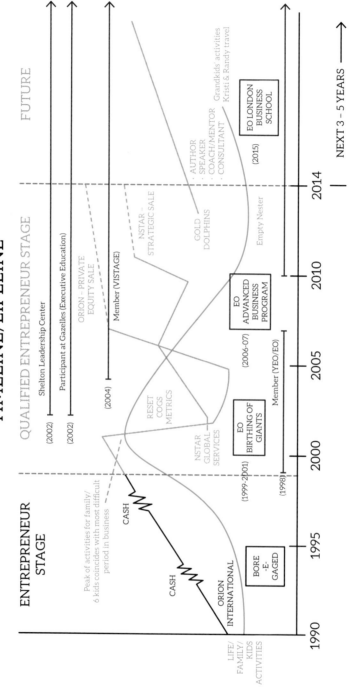

"CHECKING THE BLOCKS" QUAL CARD

Initial each requirement as met.

PREREQUISITES	INITIALS
The entrepreneur has created a Family/Personal Life timeline and overlaid it against his or her business and education timeline, looking for "takeaways" and insight.	_____
The entrepreneur has forecasted the next three to five years of the Family/Personal timeline, identifying likely points of conflict with the work of building his or her business. What "Ahas" do you see?"	_____
The entrepreneur has made a list of areas or responsibilities in his or her family life where focus and commitment are lacking, areas in which he or she is merely "checking the blocks" today.	_____
The entrepreneur has established a plan for replacing "quantity time" with "quality time."	_____

The entrepreneur acknowledges and accepts that a Qualified Entrepreneur's legacy includes all aspects of his or her life, not just those that directly pertain to starting and running a business. _____

SIGNATURE: _____

DATE: _____

Excerpt from The Third Decision _Qual Card_

THE ENTREPRENEUR QUAL CARD

Initial each requirement as met:

PREREQUISITES   INITIALS

The entrepreneur fully understands and
embraces the definition of the *Disciplined*
Entrepreneur: _____

- becomes fully self-aware that *they*
  don't know what they don't know, and
  that it's better to achieve a status
  of *"I know what I don't know."* This
  self-knowledge makes clear how the
  entrepreneur's shortcomings may be
  affecting his/her company . . . and
  usually results in a commitment to a
  lifelong learning process.   _____

- becomes fully self-aware that, for the
  business to succeed long term, a transition must occur from the business
  being about "me" as its entrepreneur/
  CEO to being about the overall needs
  of the company.   _____

· commits to undertaking the preparation necessary for making the Second
Decision. This is a conscious choice to
acquire a more disciplined approach
to management and leadership—or to
bring that discipline to the company
in another way. The *Disciplined* Entrepreneur knows that it's less important
how his/her role is shaped than that
the company excels and succeeds.
(Chapter 1)

The entrepreneur understands and
commits to the Qual Card process of self-
evaluation. (Chapter 1)

The entrepreneur takes note of the growth
phase his/her organization is at on the
Greiner Curve and the key leadership
decisions that he/she will face in the
future.[1] (Chapter 1)

Inspired by Ram Charan's challenge,
the entrepreneur commits to the work
necessary to increase his/her personal
capacity every two to three years.[2]
(Chapter 1)

The entrepreneur acknowledges that the
need to consider becoming a *Qualified
Entrepreneur* is entirely self-created,
owing to the fact that his/her successful
business now requires greater leadership
and discipline. (Chapter 2)

The entrepreneur fully understands and acknowledges the four issues that may pose a challenge to his/her efforts to become a *Qualified* Entrepreneur. Check those that apply. (Chapter 2)

- · Insistence on autonomy   _____

- · Unwillingness to build structure,
  cultivate expertise, or delegate   _____

- · Boredom   _____

- · Failure to engage in self-examination   _____

The entrepreneur fully understands the three *Qualified* Entrepreneur roles that are the possible outcomes of a Second Decision, and the two additional entrepreneur roles that represent no commitment or a limited commitment to becoming a *Qualified* Entrepreneur. The role the entrepreneur is committing to is
_____. (Chapter 2)   _____

To recognize his/her primary role in creating shareholder value, the entrepreneur has found and made copies of the company's original stock certificate(s), adding these to the QE Notebook. In addition, the entrepreneur can discuss the current and future value (three years in the future) of the organization and fully explain the trends and reasons behind the growth in stock price. (Chapter 2)   _____

The entrepreneur has drawn his/her Entrepreneurial Lifeline, beginning with the start date of the first entrepreneurial venture and including all businesses that have followed. The lifeline should be a graphic representation of the highs and lows in his/her career, and include an extension out three to five years into the future. (Chapter 3) _____

The entrepreneur has created an economic graph to indicate macroeconomic and industry-specific trends during the span of the lifeline. (Chapter 3) _____

The entrepreneur has imagined himself/herself explaining the lifeline and the career it represents to a small group of entrepreneurial peers. (Chapter 3) _____

The entrepreneur has gone online to take the PRF (Personality Research Form), obtained a complete printout, and placed a copy in the QE Notebook. In addition, here is the link for taking the Myers-Briggs. See: https://www.mbticomplete.com/en/index.aspx. (Chapter 4) _____

The entrepreneur has become familiar with the four types of CEO leadership introduced in this chapter: Urgent/Reactive, Ever Optimistic, Reflexively Pessimistic, and Steady/Proactive. The entrepreneur has assessed which type or types pertain to him/her in various contexts of leadership, recognizing that while some types will predominate, few if any CEOs will fit just one category. (Chapter 4) _____

The entrepreneur has listed the three to five major changes that a replacement CEO would make to his/her company within 12 months of taking over, and offered a full explanation as to why the changes would be implemented, as well as why the current CEO is not making those changes. The entrepreneur has placed a copy of this analysis in the QE Notebook. (Chapter 5)   _____

The entrepreneur has set one-year and three-year goals for the company and put them in writing in the QE Notebook. (Chapter 5)   _____

The entrepreneur has evaluated his/her performance in visioning, using the A to F scale in the chart from this chapter and added a copy to the QE Notebook. The entrepreneur understands the level and depth of knowledge expected of the CEO by his/her accountability partner (the board of directors, coaches, consultants, or advisers) in regards to the three-year vision for the organization. (Chapter 5)   _____

The entrepreneur can fully explain his/her visioning process for the future and has a plan in place to achieve a performance rating of A when visioning is complete. (Chapter 5)   _____

The entrepreneur has become fully self-aware of the people who should be included in the visioning process and how visioning meetings or retreats should be structured for best results. (Chapter 5) ....

The entrepreneur understands and embraces the "No Year Two Allowed" policy, understanding the reasons why it improves visioning and planning. (Chapter 5) ....

The entrepreneur has committed to establishing discipline, starting by choosing and implementing an accountability and execution system for their organization and completing the *One-Page Strategic Plan*, putting a copy in the QE Notebook. (Chapter 6) _____

The entrepreneur fully accepts his/her own accountability leadership responsibilities, absolving employees and direct reports of fault until disciplined thinking is embraced at the CEO level. (Chapter 6) _____

The entrepreneur has committed to establishing discipline, starting with making the key leadership decision of who will own the execution/accountability system— the CEO or the COO/Operations leader. (Chapter 6) _____

The entrepreneur fully understands that discipline is synonymous with self-control and to some extent a substitute for motivation. (Chapter 6) _____

The entrepreneur has become fully self-aware of his/her personality type in relation to managing cash (Urgent/ Reactive, Ever Optimistic, Reflexively Pessimistic, or Steady/Proactive). (Chapter 7) _____

The entrepreneur has developed a regimen for forecasting cash needs monthly and at least six months in advance, and is receiving a daily cash report. (Chapter 7) _____

The entrepreneur has developed a regimen for forecasting the organization's financial covenants at least six months in advance to predict and prevent breaches. (Chapter 7) _____

After personally reviewing the new Six Months' Cash and Covenants forecast each month, the entrepreneur has made it a practice to compare the next quarter's goals with the forecast to ensure there are no glaring conflicts between goals, availability of cash, and the ability to stay in acceptable range of the business's financial covenants. This review is done with full regard to the capital expenditures (personnel, equipment, etc.) that are planned but not yet made. (Chapter 7) _____

The entrepreneur has made the CFO/ accounting manager decision, thus ensuring that a designated financial position exists to either assist or lead the task of tracking cash in the business. (Chapter 7)

_____

The entrepreneur has added to the QE Notebook three items: the signed personal guarantee forms from the bank and up-to-date Six Months' Cash and Covenants forecasts. (Chapter 7)

_____

The entrepreneur has committed to operating the business with COGS—Cost of Goods Sold—as a focus, fully recognizing that every dollar of COGS savings is equal to one dollar of profit. The entrepreneur understands that the _intent_ for defining COGS as all expenses is to get him/her to understand each of them, rather than to change commonly used terminology in accounting. (Chapter 8)

_____

The entrepreneur has completed a historical three-year financial COGS chart, including two tables—numbers-only and percentages-only—and the input includes all of the line items from the company income statement and their values. (Chapter 8)

_____

The entrepreneur is able to fully explain the Table 2 percentage charts, as if going through a "check-out" process. This includes describing in detail the trends in COGS percentages over the past three years, while also establishing and explaining the reasoning behind the budget set-point for the current fiscal year in the Table 3 chart. (Chapter 8)

_____

The entrepreneur has converted the budget COGS expense percentage targets to numbers, based on the fiscal year revenue goal, and has made necessary adjustments to come up with the final approved budget. (Chapter 8)

_____

Monthly, the entrepreneur is measuring and reviewing actual-versus-target for the current fiscal year budget, both numbers and percentages. (Chapter 8)

_____

The entrepreneur has placed the three-year COGS reports into the QE Notebook. (Chapter 8)

_____

The entrepreneur has compiled a list of all metrics currently used or monitored in the business in a spreadsheet, adding a column for naming the person accountable for setting baseline data for each metric. (Chapter 9)

_____

The entrepreneur has compiled a (minimum) three-year report on the metrics in his/her business pertaining to Payroll COGS and Employee Productivity (both at the company and salesperson levels) and set targets for the current fiscal year. The entrepreneur is using these two reports as a training ground, embracing the trend analysis and decision making that occurs while completing this exercise, and adding additional customized metrics to the three-year metric report. (Chapter 9) _____

The entrepreneur has added the three-year metric and Payroll COGS report to the QE Notebook. (Chapter 9) _____

The entrepreneur has established a minimum of three and as many as five company-level leading indicator metrics that are specific to his/her business. (Chapter 9) _____

The entrepreneur has researched and determined market data for his/her business's industry, to include overall market size, three-year projections to track trends, and market-share data for top competitors. (Chapter 9) _____

The entrepreneur has conducted an audit of his/her company's core values to ensure they are actively influential in company policies and that the people of the organization live by them. (Chapter 10) _____

The entrepreneur has developed his/her
own personal value statements.
(Chapter 10)   _____

The entrepreneur has established consistent and company-wide training on the
business's core values and has communicated to employees that decisions to hire,
fire, train, and promote will be based on
adherence to these core values.
(Chapter 10)   _____

The entrepreneur has made a list of past
decisions that have been consistent with
maintaining core values and have caused
a direct financial hit on the business.
(Chapter 10)   _____

The entrepreneur has made a list of the
kinds of decisions he/she may need to
make, noting potential conflict between
the company's revenue growth and its core
values. From this a list of possible actions
and responses has been developed, that is,
"If this happens, I would do this."
(Chapter 10)   _____

The entrepreneur has become fully self-aware that "I don't know what I don't know" (IDKWIDK), and that it's better to achieve a status of "I know what I don't know" (IKWIDK). This self-knowledge has revealed how the entrepreneur's short-comings may be affecting his/her company and has resulted in a commitment to a life-long learning process. (Chapter 11)

The entrepreneur has developed his/her Entrepreneurial Education Lifeline and overlaid it with the Career/Profes-sional Lifeline created early in the book, looking for any "aha moments" that may be observed in his/her career to date. Both have been extended out three to five years in the future. (Chapter 11)

The entrepreneur has committed to increasing his/her personal capacity. To that end, he/she has listed the entrepre-neurial education methods to be utilized in the next 12 months (choosing from the Accountability, Consultation, and Teaching options). (Chapter 11)

The entrepreneur has determined where he/she falls on the bored/engaged scale and why. (Chapter 12)

The entrepreneur has assessed his/her leadership personality (Urgent/Reactive, Ever Optimistic, Reflexively Pessimistic, or Steady/Proactive) with regard to serial entrepreneurship and bor-e-gagement. (Chapter 12)

        ————————————

The entrepreneur has reviewed the businesses that he/she has started, and has evaluated how bor-e-gagement prompted startups of new companies or contributed to business failures. (Chapter 12)

        ————————————

The entrepreneur has conducted the self-examination necessary to determine whether he/she is running the current business for the benefit of an entrepreneurial ego or for the long-term success of the company and its employees. (Chapter 12)

        ————————————

The entrepreneur has developed a list of actions that would need to be taken to ready his/her current business for a transition to new leadership, should he/she elect to move on to a new startup. (Chapter 12)

        ————————————

The entrepreneur has created a "real budget"—one that represents where he/she really expects to be based on current industry and macroeconomic trends—and done all planning around this budget. (Chapter 13)

        ————————————

The entrepreneur has created a "success budget" for the possibility that the company will over-produce and hit even its stretch targets, and asked himself/herself to consider what sorts of resources will be required in this scenario. (This should truly be a best-case scenario budget, not the everyday budget of an over-optimistic entrepreneur.) (Chapter 13) _____

The entrepreneur has created a contingency-to-crisis budget to prepare, as the US Navy does, for the worst-case scenario. This budget considers potential expense cuts to handle revenue reductions of 10, 20, 30 percent or whatever alternate percentages the entrepreneur prefers. Being a theoretical exercise only, showing the entrepreneur's plan for keeping the ship afloat in any weather, conditions or circumstances; this could also be termed a "peace-of-mind" budget. (Chapter 13) _____

The entrepreneur has created a "no-layoff" budget to war-game an attempt to keep the company profitable in a downturn without downsizing the workforce. This budget, aimed primarily at those who have taken a no-layoffs pledge, requires the entrepreneur to use a COGS analysis to identify expense-cutting options that do not affect personnel. (Chapter 13) _____

To complete his/her training in the area
of contingency planning, crisis leadership, and the RESET button, the *Qualified*
Entrepreneur has assured himself/herself
that he/she is:

_____

- ready to write the company's sequel, if
  need be, through the use of the RESET
  button;

- prepared to face consequences for
  making decisions that need to be made;

- well-prepared for adversity before
  it occurs, having scheduled contingency planning/training on an annual
  basis, including leadership training at
  various levels of the organization; and

- accepting of change—aware that it is
  inevitable, and confident of being able
  to handle it and find opportunity in it.
  (Chapter 13)

_____

The entrepreneur has imagined the "Day
of the Wire" and spent time taking stock of
how he/she is likely to feel at such a major
career inflection point. This includes considering what the company's value may
be, what structural and strategic decisions
have contributed to its valuation, and
how leading this company has affected
the entrepreneur's family/personal life.
(Chapter 14)

_____

Using advice from experienced entrepreneurs, the entrepreneur has identified any
changes he/she may wish to make—either
inside the company or to his/her life
balance—before reaching the Day of the
Wire. (Chapter 14)   _____

In preparation for filling out a final assessment of all Qual Cards within this book,
the entrepreneur has established whether
he/she is leading a growth company or a
lifestyle business and whether the type
identified matches the entrepreneur's own
life and career goals. (Chapter 14)   _____

The entrepreneur fully commits to continuous career-long learning and doubling
his/her personal capacity every three
years, acknowledging that the Qual Card
process is just the beginning . . .   _____

_____

The entrepreneur has created a Family/
Personal Life timeline and overlaid it
against his or her business and education
timeline, looking for "takeaways" and
insight. (*The Third Decision*)   _____

The entrepreneur has forecasted the next
three to five years of the Family/Personal
timeline, identifying likely points of
conflict with the work of building his or
her business. What "Ahas" do you see?"
(*The Third Decision*)   _____

The entrepreneur has made a list of areas
or responsibilities in his or her family
life where focus and commitment are
lacking, areas in which he or she is merely
"checking the blocks" today. (*The Third
Decision*)

      ——————————

The entrepreneur has established a plan
for replacing "quantity time" with "quality
time." (*The Third Decision*)

      ——————————

The entrepreneur acknowledges and
accepts that a Qualified Entrepreneur's
legacy includes all aspects of his or her
life, not just those that directly pertain to
starting and running a business. (*The Third
Decision*)

      ——————————

THE SEAWATER QUESTION ANSWERED!

Back in Chapter One, I posed a question from my navy days:

"I am a drop of seawater about to enter the submarine. Explain how I turn the light on over your bed when you're done with your work and want to read a book."

So how does that drop of seawater actually turn on the light over a seaman's bunk?

The technical answer is below, provided by my friend and fellow US Navy submariner, Captain Dan Forney. Dan is a Naval Academy graduate and was a classmate of mine during my nuclear power training. Dan served as commanding officer of two nuclear submarines and also as the commander of the US Navy's largest fleet training center.

Q. How does a drop of seawater make your bunk light come on?

A. Seawater is all around your submarine. It keeps the ship afloat and provides the medium through which the ship moves. Seawater also supplies a vital resource to keep the ship operating at sea for extended periods of time. It provides fresh water for the crew's use (cooking, drinking, and washing), fresh water for the propulsion plant (both the reactor and the steam plant), and it even provides oxygen for the crew to breathe, which allows the submarine to remain closed to the outside atmosphere for extended periods of time.

In order for a drop of seawater to make your bunk light illuminate it must undergo some preparation first. The seawater is taken into the submarine through an auxiliary seawater system. It is piped to the ship's evaporator where it is boiled. The evaporator is a steam-heated distilling plant that boils seawater. When seawater boils, the steam is pure water with none of the salt that is in the seawater left over. The pure steam is piped to a condenser where it is returned to a liquid state and pumped to wherever it is needed, now as pure water. If the crew needs more fresh water, the evaporator condensate is sent to the ship's potable water tanks. If the propulsion plant requires makeup water, the evaporator distillate is sent to the reserve feedwater tanks through the propulsion plant demineralizer. The propulsion plant demineralizer is a resin bed that deionizes the water and provides a final filtration. The result is extremely pure water that is suitable for use in the propulsion plant boilers—called steam generators in a nuclear power plant.

In a naval pressurized water reactor plant, the reactor is cooled by water in a closed system that is circulated in the reactor's primary cooling loop. The primary water passes through the reactor core where it is heated and then goes to the steam generator where it passes through heat exchanger tubes. The heat is transferred through the tube to the secondary plant water on the other side of the tubes inside the steam generator. This water boils and creates steam to propel the ship and to make electricity.

Once our drop of water is in the reserve feedwater tank, it is ready for use when needed. When the water level in the main condenser drops to a set level, an automatic valve opens and vacuum drags water from the reserve feed tank into the condenser. The main propulsion condenser operates at a vacuum, so it provides a natural motive force to move water from the vented reserve feed tank into the condenser. Our drop of water is pumped from the condenser by the condensate pump to the suction of the main feed pump. The water is then pumped from the main feed pump into the steam generator. In the steam generator this secondary plant water is heated to boiling by the hotter primary plant water inside the heat exchanger tubes.

The pressure on the secondary side of the steam generator is lower than the pressure on the primary side, so the water on the secondary side will boil and create steam. This steam is the main propulsion steam. The drop of water, now in the form of steam, is routed through the main steam system to various functions, the most important of which are to propel the ship and to provide electricity for the ship's use. Our drop of water will pass through the electrical generator throttle valve and then into the ship's electrical generator turbine causing the generator to spin and generate electricity. The water then passes into the main condenser where it is condensed at a vacuum and is ready to begin its journey to the steam generator again.

The electricity produced is available for use by all of the electrical devices on the ship, from pumps, to controls, to the galley, and even to your bunk light. So when you turn on your bunk light, it is really a drop of seawater that allows you to read in comfort!

APPENDIX D

LINE OFFICER SUBMARINE QUAL CARD (EXCERPT)

COMSUBLANTINST 1552.6D
COMSUBPACINST 1552.1J

1 0 FEB 1983

LINE OFFICER SUBMARINE
QUALIFICATION CARD

Name RANDALL H. NELSON   Reporting Date 26 NOV 1984

A. PREREQUISITES

	*Signature	Date
⊠ 1. Qualified as Diving Officer of the Watch.	_(signature)_	28 OCT 85
2. Qualified as Officer of the Deck (surfaced and submerged).	_(signature)_	11 JUN 1986
3. Qualified as Duty Officer.	_(signature)_	6/14/86
4. Qualified as Engineering Officer of the Watch (nuclear trained officers).	_(signature)_	5 AUG 85
5. Qualified as Engineering Duty Officer (nuclear trained officers).	_(signature)_	5 AUG 85
6. Qualified as Weapons Duty Officer (SSBN officers who have completed the Weapons Officer course at NAVGMSCOL, Dam Neck/TRITRAFAC, Bangor).	N/A	N/A
7. Meets the minimum time requirements as established in the basic instruction.	_(signature)_	15 NOV 85

B. KNOWLEDGE REQUIREMENTS

1. Discuss the following submarine force mission concepts and operations: _(signature)_ 6/12/86

    a. Approach

    b. Attack

    c. Opposing ASW ships and screens

    d. Coordinated Tactics/Direct Support

*Signatures must be from an officer qualified in submarines. If the designated officer is not qualified, that officer's department head will sign.

Enclosure (8)

COMSUBLANTINST 1552.6D
COMSUBPACINST 1552.1J

10 FEB 1983

*Signature   Date

  e. Mining

  f. Photo-reconnaissance

  g. Swimmer operations

  h. Strategic deterrence

  i. Transitors

  j. Anti-submarine operations

  k. Reconnaissance/intelligence/surveillance

  l. Landing and recovery of personnel

  m. Under ice operations

  n. Search and rescue

  o. Blockade and Quarantine

  p. Navigational and hydrographic data collection

  q. MEDEVAC and HUMEVAC

 2. Characteristics of Soviet Surface
Warships and Aircraft including Initial
Detection and Contact Evasions   *M.C. Carter* *2 June 86*

  Ref: 4, 21, 22, 55, 66, 91, 92, 127

  a. Explain the visual, ESM and
Sonar recognition and classification
techniques for Soviet surface warships
and aircraft.

  b. Discuss the expected initial
acoustic detection range for Soviet
surface warships based upon their radiated
noise and active sonars.

  3. Strategic Weapons Systems Capabilities (if applicable)   *signature* *8 Jul 86*
               Weapons Officer

  Ref: 6, 30, 31, 80, 81, 112, 113

Enclosure (8)   2

COMSUBLANTINST 1552.6D
COMSUBPACINST 1552.1J

1 0 FEB 1983

*Signature   Date

8. Stability: Longitudinal and Transverse

Ref: 29, 31, 65

a. Demonstrate a thorough knowledge of the equilibrium polygon with respect to buoyancy and ship control.

9. Approach and Attack Tactics

Ref: 75

a. For each of the following Battle Stations Supervisory positions, discuss with that supervisor his duties, responsibilities, considerations, and recommendations for the indicated situations:

(1) Own ship maneuvers

Sonar Supervisor (Officer)

(2) Weapons and tube preparations

Torpedo Room Supervisor

(3) Primary target maneuvers

Weapons Control Coordinator

(4) Secondary target detection and tracking

Plot Coordinator

(5) Periscope observations

Officer of the Deck

(6) Firing Point Procedures

Fire Control Coordinator

(7) Post launch target and weapons tracking

Fire Control Coordinator

(8) Post launch evolutions

Fire Control Coordinator

5   Enclosure (8)

COMSUBLANTINST 1552.6D
COMSUBPACINST 1552.1J
1 0 FEB 1983

*Signature   Date

Oral examination results
(4.0 scale) ___3.4___

Senior Watch Officer ___12 June 86___

3. The candidate has demonstrated a
temperament suitable for submarine
duty, has completed an oral examination
and is recommended for qualification in
submarines.

Oral examination results
(4.0 scale) ___3.6___

Executive Officer ___6/13/86___

4. The candidate has completed
an oral examination and is recommended
for qualification in submarines.

Commanding Officer ___6/14/86___

Enclosure (8)   14

NOTES

CHAPTER 1: WHAT IS THE SECOND DECISION?

1. Zweig, Jason. "Charles Munger: Secrets of Buffett's Success." http://blogs.wsj.com/moneybeat/2014/09/12/the-secrets-of-berkshire-hathaways-success-an-interview-with-charlie-munger/

2. U.S. Department of Labor. "Bureau of Labor and Statistics: Entrepreneurship and the Economy." http://www.bls.gov/bdm/entrepreneurship/bdm_chart3.htm.

3. Small Business Administration Office of Advocacy. "Frequently Asked Questions." http://www.sba.gov/sites/default/files/FAQ_Sept_2012.pdf.

4. Thean, Patrick. "The How of Growth." Gazelles Systems Rhythm Blog, January 21, 2014. http://www.rhythmsystems.com/blog/bid/155871/The-How-of-Growth.

5. Peric, Kosta. "The Three Best Job Titles of 2012." *Forbes*, December 28, 2012. http://www.forbes.com/sites/kostaperic/2012/12/28/the-three-best-job-titles-of-2012-and-a-wish-for-2013/.

6. Elmer, Vickie. "Moving Mountains: The Problem with Calling Your Career Coach a 'Sherpa.'" *Quartz*, October 5, 2013. http://qz.com/128842/the-problem-with-calling-your-career-coach-a-sherpa/.

7. Farrell, Rachel. "Workplace Issues: 13 Unusual Job Titles." *Careerbuilder*, July 7, 2010. http://www.careerbuilder.com/Article/CB-1712-Workplace-Issues-13-Unusual-Job-Titles.

8. Giang, Vivian. "Recruiting Firm Shares the 50 Weirdest Job Titles They've Ever Seen." *Business Insider*, August 16, 2012. http://www.

businessinsider.com/recruiting-firm-shares-the-50-weirdest-job-titles-theyve-ever-seen-2012-8#ixzz3CwSl107p.

9. Mason, Lacey. "Why Witty Job Titles Are All the Rage." *Brazen Life*, November 21, 2011. http://blog.brazencareerist.com/2011/11/21/why-witty-job-titles-are-all-the-rage/.

10. Organic Valley. "George Siemon: C-E-I-E-I-O." http://www.organicvalley.coop/newsroom/about-organic-valley/our-ceo/

11. Springhetti, Jim. "Oregon Companies Having Fun with Job Titles." *The Oregonian*, January 13, 2009. http://www.oregonlive.com/business/index.ssf/2009/01/oregon_companies_having_fun_wi.html.

12. MindTools. " The Greiner Curve: Surviving the Crises That Come With Growth." http://www.mindtools.com/pages/article/newLDR_87.htm

13. Thean, Patrick. "The How of Growth." Gazelles Systems Rhythm Blog, January 21, 2014. http://www.rhythmsystems.com/blog/bid/155871/The-How-of-Growth.

CHAPTER 2: THE CHALLENGE OF STARTUP SUCCESS

1. Buchanan, Leigh. "What Drives Entrepreneurs?" *Inc.*, February 28, 2012. http://www.inc.com/magazine/201203/motivation-matrix.html.

2. Small Business Administration Office of Advocacy. "Frequently Asked Questions." http://www.sba.gov/sites/default/files/FAQ_Sept_2012.pdf.

3. U.S. Department of Labor. "Bureau of Labor and Statistics: Entrepreneurship and the Economy." http://www.bls.gov/bdm/entrepreneurship/bdm_chart3.htm.

4. Collins, Jim and Jerry I. Porras. *Built to Last: Successful Habits of Visionary Companies*. New York: Harper Business, 1994.

CHAPTER 4: WHAT KIND OF LEADER ARE YOU?

1. The Myers & Briggs Foundation. "MBTI® Basics." http://www.myers-briggs.org/my-mbti-personality-type/mbti-basics/home.htm

2. Disc Personality Testing. "Use these disc Peronality Tests to Increase Your Professional and Personal Success." http://discpersonalitytesting.com

3. SIGMA Assessment Systems, Inc. "Personality Research Form." http://sigmaassessmentsystems.com/assessments/prf.asp

4. Covey, Stephen R. *The 7 Habits of Highly Effective People: Powerful Lessons in Personal Change.* New York: Simon & Shuster, 1990.

CHAPTER 5: HOW TO DEVELOP AND
BRIEF YOUR THREE-YEAR VISION

1. Collins, Jim and Jerry I. Porras. *Built to Last: Successful Habits of Visionary Companies.* New York: Harper Business, 1994.

2. Adams, Susan. "New Survey: Majority of Employees Dissatisfied." *Forbes*, May 18, 2012. http://www.forbes.com/sites/susanadams/2012/05/18/new-survey-majority-of-employees-dissatisfied/.

3. "One in Five Workers Plan to Change Jobs in 2014, According to CareerBuilder Survey." *Careerbuilder*, January 9, 2014. http://www.careerbuilder.com/share/aboutus/pressreleasesdetail.aspx?sd=1%2F9%2F2014&id=pr797&ed=12%2F31%2F2014.

4. Hall, Alan. "I'm Outta Here: Why 2 Million Americans Quit Every Month and Five Steps to Turn the Epidemic Around." *Forbes*, March 3, 2013. http://www.forbes.com/sites/alanhall/2013/03/11/im-outta-here-why-2-million-americans-quit-every-month-and-5-steps-to-turn-the-epidemic-around/.

5. Weber, Peter. "Why Most Americans Hate Their Jobs or are Just Checked Out." *The Week*, June 25, 2013. http://theweek.com/article/index/246084/why-most-americans-hate-their-jobs-or-are-just-checked-out.

6. Buchanan, Leigh. "35 Great Questions." *Inc.*, April 2014. http://www.incmagazine-digital.com/incmagazine/201404?pg=104#pg104.

CHAPTER 6: EXECUTION: GOALS AND ACCOUNTABILITY

1. Discipline. n.d. http://www.thefreedictionary.com/discipline *(accessed September 12, 2014).*

2. Discipline. n.d. http://*en.wikipedia.org/wiki/Discipline (accessed September 12, 2014).*

3. Goltz, Jay. "Top 10 Reasons Businesses Fail." You're the Boss: The Art of Running a Small Business blog. *The New York Times,* January 5, 2011. http://boss.blogs.nytimes.com/2011/01/05/top-10-reasons-small-businesses-fail/?_php=true&_type=blogs&_r=0.

CHAPTER 7: SIX MONTHS' CASH AND COVENANTS

1. "Cash Flow." n.d. *Dun and Bradstreet Small Business.,* http://dnbsmallbusiness.com.au/Cash_Flow/ (accessed September 12, 2014.)

2. Peavler, Rosemary. "Cash Management is Important for Your Small Business." About Money blog, n.d. http://bizfinance.about.com/od/cashmanagement/a/cash_mngt.htm.

3. Goltz, Jay. "Top 10 Reasons Businesses Fail." You're the Boss: The Art of Running a Small Business blog. *The New York Times,* January 5, 2011. http://boss.blogs.nytimes.com/2011/01/05/top-10-reasons-small-businesses-fail/?_php=true&_type=blogs&_r=0.

4. Ibid.

5. Accounting Manager Job Description. n.d. https://www.kforce.com/salaryguide/2014/fa/job-descriptions/. (Accessed September 12, 2014.)

6. Chief Financial Officer Job Description. n.d. http://www.ehow.com/careers/. (Accessed September 12, 2014.)

CHAPTER 8: COGS-NIZANCE: PROFIT AND EXPENSE LEADERSHIP

1. Goltz, Jay. "Top 10 Reasons Businesses Fail." You're the Boss: The Art of Running a Small Business blog. *The New York Times,*

January 5, 2011. http://boss.blogs.nytimes.com/2011/01/05/
top-10-reasons-small-businesses-fail/?_php=true&_type=blogs&_r=0.

CHAPTER 9: METRICS: MINING FOR GOLD

1. Lewis, Michael. *Moneyball: The Art of Winning an Unfair Game.* New York: W.W. Norton and Company, 2003.

2. Kramers, Kraig. *CEO Tools: The Nuts-N-Bolts for Every Manager's Success.* Stockbridge, GA: Gandy Dancer Press, 2002.

3. Olsen, Erica. "Strategic Planning: The Trailing 12 Months Chart." *Strategic Planning Kit for Dummies, 2nd Edition.* http://www.dummies.com/how-to/content/strategic-planning-the-trailing-12-months-chart.html.

CHAPTER 10: VALUES-BASED LEADERSHIP

1. Core values. n.d. http://examples.yourdictionary.com/examples-of-core-values.html. (Accessed September 12, 2014.)

2. Jansen Kramer, Harry M. Jr. "The Only True Leadership Is Values-Based Leadership." *Forbes*, April 26, 2011. http://www.forbes.com/2011/04/26/values-based-leadership.html.

3. Jansen Kramer, Harry M. Jr . "How to Be a Values-Based Leader In Times Of Trial." *Forbes*, June 14, 2011. http://www.forbes.com/2011/06/14/values-based-leadership.html.

4. Jansen Kramer, Harry M. Jr. *From Values to Action: The Four Principles of Values-Based Leadership.* San Francisco: Jossey-Bass, 2011.

5. Collins, Jim and Jerry I. Porras. *Built to Last: Successful Habits of Visionary Companies.* New York: Harper Business, 1994.

6. Zappos.com, Inc. Code of Business Conduct and Ethics. May 1, 2010. http://www.zappos.com/c/code-of-conduct. (Accessed September 12, 2014.)

7. Siltanen, Rob. "The Real Story Behind Apple's 'Think Different' Campaign." *Forbes*, December 14, 2011.

http://www.forbes.com/sites/onmarketing/2011/12/14/
the-real-story-behind-apples-think-different-campaign/.

8. Ben and Jerry's: Issues We Care About. http://www.benjerry.com/values/
    issues-we-care-about. (Accessed September 12, 2014.)

9. Patagonia: Our Reason for Being. http://www.patagonia.com/us/
    patagonia.go?assetid=2047. (Accessed September 12, 2014.)

10. Don't be evil. n.d. http://en.wikipedia.org/wiki/Don%27t_be_evil.
    (Accessed September 12, 2014.)

11. Martin, Timothy W. and Mike Esterl. "CVS to Stop Selling Cigarettes."
    Wall Street Journal, February 5, 2014. http://online.wsj.com/news/
    articles/SB10001424052702304851104579363520905849600.

12. Jansen Kramer, Harry M. Jr. "The Only True Leadership Is Values-Based
    Leadership." *Forbes*, April 26, 2011. http://www.forbes.com/2011/04/26/
    values-based-leadership.html.

13. Jansen Kramer, Harry M. Jr . "How to Be a Values-Based Leader
    In Times Of Trial." *Forbes*, June 14, 2011. http://www.forbes.
    com/2011/06/14/values-based-leadership.html.

14. Jansen Kramer, Harry M. Jr. *From Values to Action: The Four Principles of
    Values-Based Leadership.* San Francisco: Jossey-Bass, 2011.

15. Cooper, Helene. "92 Air Force Officers Suspended for Cheating on Their
    Missile Exam." *New York Times*, January 30, 2014. http://www.nytimes.
    com/2014/01/31/us/politics/92-air-force-officers-suspended-for-cheat-
    ing-on-their-missile-exam.html?_r=0.

16. List of corporate collapses and scandals. n.d. http://en.wikipedia.org/
    wiki/List_of_corporate_collapses_and_scandals. (Accessed September 12,
    2014.

17. Vanden Brook, Tom. "Senators blast Army over recruit-
    ing fraud scandal." *USA Today*, February 4, 2014. http://
    www.usatoday.com/story/news/nation/2014/02/04/
    national-guard-recruiting-kickbacks-scandal/5200993/.

18. Jansen Kramer, Harry M. Jr. "The Only True Leadership Is Values-Based Leadership." *Forbes*, April 26, 2011. http://www.forbes.com/2011/04/26/values-based-leadership.html.

19. Jansen Kramer, Harry M. Jr . "How to Be a Values-Based Leader In Times Of Trial." *Forbes*, June 14, 2011. http://www.forbes.com/2011/06/14/values-based-leadership.html.

20. Jansen Kramer, Harry M. Jr. *From Values to Action: The Four Principles of Values-Based Leadership.* San Francisco: Jossey-Bass, 2011.

CHAPTER 11: CAREER-LONG LEARNING

1. Shelton Leadership Center, Raleigh N.C. Web page of NC State. http://sheltonleadership.ncsu.edu/.

CHAPTER 12: BOR-E-GAGED

1. Pet Shop Boys. Youtube.com video. https://www.youtube.com/watch?v=InBiaRBUjUs.

2. Small Business Administration Office of Advocacy. "Frequently Asked Questions." http://www.sba.gov/sites/default/files/FAQ_Sept_2012.pdf

3. U.S. Department of Labor. "Bureau of Labor and Statistics: Entrepreneurship and the Economy." http://www.bls.gov/bdm/entrepreneurship/bdm_chart3.htm

4. *Fortune.* "How Long is Too Long or Too Short For a CEO to Lead?" October 23, 2012. http://fortune.com/2012/10/23/how-long-is-too-long-or-too-short-for-a-ceo-to-lead/.

CHAPTER 13: CRISIS LEADERSHIP, CONTINGENCY PLANNING AND THE RESET BUTTON

1. Simmons AN, Fitzpatrick S, Strigo IA, Potterat EG, Johnson DC, Matthews SC, Van Orden KF, Swain JL, Paulus MP (2012). Altered insula activation in anticipation of changing emotional states: neural mechanisms underlying cognitive flexibility in special operations forces personnel. *Neuroreport: Cognitive Neuroscience and Neuropsychology.*

2. Sullivan, Andrew. "Anticipating the Strain," *The Dish* blog. January 8, 2014, 7:31 AM.

3. Small Business Administration Office of Advocacy. "Frequently Asked Questions." http://www.sba.gov/sites/default/files/FAQ_Sept_2012.pdf

4. U.S. Department of Labor. "Bureau of Labor and Statistics: Entrepreneurship and the Economy." http://www.bls.gov/bdm/entrepreneurship/bdm_chart3.htm

5. Sullivan, Andrew. "Anticipating the Strain," *The Dish* blog. January 8, 2014, 7:31 AM.

6. Davis, Kathleen. "Jim Collins on Creative Discipline, Paranoia and Other Marks of a Great Leader." *Entrepreneur*, October 3, 2012. http://www.entrepreneur.com/article/224568.

7. Jansen Kramer, Harry M. Jr. "The Only True Leadership Is Values-Based Leadership." *Forbes*, April 26, 2011. http://www.forbes.com/2011/04/26/values-based-leadership.html.

8. Jansen Kramer, Harry M. Jr . "How to Be a Values-Based Leader In Times Of Trial." *Forbes*, June 14, 2011. http://www.forbes.com/2011/06/14/values-based-leadership.html.

9. Jansen Kramer, Harry M. Jr. *From Values to Action: The Four Principles of Values-Based Leadership.* San Francisco: Jossey-Bass, 2011.

CHAPTER 14: REFLECTION: PEER ADVICE AND INSIGHTS

1. Ware, Bronnie. *The Top Five Regrets of the Dying: A Life Transformed by the Dearly Departing.* Hay House, 2011.

CHAPTER 15: THE SECOND DECISION

1. Clifton, Jim and Sangeeta Bharadwaj Badal. *Entrepreneurial Strengths-Finder.* New York: Gallup Press, 2014.

2. Goltz, Jay. "Top 10 Reasons Businesses Fail." You're the Boss: The Art of Running a Small Business blog. *The New York Times,*

January 5, 2011. http://boss.blogs.nytimes.com/2011/01/05/
top-10-reasons-small-businesses-fail/?_php=true&_type=blogs&_r=0.

3. Myatt, Mike. "Businesses Don't Fail – Leaders Do." *Forbes*, January
    12, 2012. http://www.forbes.com/sites/mikemyatt/2012/01/12/
    businesses-dont-fail-leaders-do/.

4. Surowiecki, James. "Epic Fails of the Startup World." *The New Yorker*,
    May 19, 2014. http://www.newyorker.com/magazine/2014/05/19/
    epic-fails-of-the-startup-world.

5. Thean, Patrick. "The How of Growth." Gazelles Systems Rhythm Blog,
    January 21, 2014. http://www.rhythmsystems.com/blog/bid/155871/
    The-How-of-Growth.

APPENDIX B: THE ENTREPRENEUR'S QUAL CARD

1. MindTools. "The Greiner Curve: Surviving the Crises That Come With
    Growth." http://www.mindtools.com/pages/article/newLDR_87.htm

2. Thean, Patrick. "The How of Growth." Gazelles Systems Rhythm Blog,
    January 21, 2014. http://www.rhythmsystems.com/blog/bid/155871/
    The-How-of-Growth.

BACK COVER

1. Thomas, G. Scott. "144K U.S. businesses fit into medium classifica-
    tion." http://www.bizjournals.com/bizjournals/on-numbers/scott-
    thomas/2011/11/144k-us-businesses-fit-into-medium.html.

2. Thomas, G. Scott. "Almost 98% of all businesses are classified as small
    businesses." http://www.bizjournals.com/bizjournals/on-numbers/scott-
    thomas/2011/11/98-of-all-businesses-are-small.html.

THANK YOU'S

In 2011, I was honored to receive the Admiral Sidney Souers Distinguished Alumni Award at my alma mater, Miami University in Oxford, Ohio. As I prepared my speech to accept the award, it became crystal clear to me that I did not get to this place in my life without the significant help and guidance of many others. I have tried to do my best to expound that list below. I am forever grateful to each and every one of you.

Kristi, you are my wife, my best friend, and my biggest supporter. (And I am yours!) I am simply a better person, husband, and father because of you.

Nicole/Glen, Shannon/Silas, Katie/Matt, Mike, Matt, and Maggie—now that you are grown adults, I can sit back and passively watch (and smile!) as you create your own paths in life, utilizing your strengths in your own unique ways. I am a very proud and lucky dad!

Connor, Foster, Cameron, and Avery, Papa Ry simply loves his time with his grandsons (and Nana does, too.) Kids, please make more and how about a few granddaughters, too.

Mom and Dad, I am who I am because of you. You taught me exceedingly well and I am forever grateful. Now I truly understand your parenting strategy of high standards and high love. It certainly worked.

Jeff and Tom Nelson, you taught me how to play, compete, and win as a team. You have been role models to me and provided the motivation, support, and fierce competitive fire that I carry with me today.

To each one of my friends and family members, you have truly taught me that life is not just about work. I plan on continuing to find ways to enjoy our time together and hope you will do the same; laughing, having fun, and supporting each other through good and bad times.

John, David and Greg, you have taught me that no matter what our goals and dreams are, it's our health that dictates how we live our lives and for how long. Thank you for your friendship and for providing me with perspective. I hope I can live my life in a way that will make you proud.

Bill Laughlin, my great 30-year friend and Orion business partner, I am proud of what we accomplished together—it clearly was 1+1 = much more than 3. When I say "I" in this book, it also reads as "we". It was a heck of a ride and we were a powerful team together!

Jim Tully, our ride together at Orion was a bit shorter but just as meaningful. Thank you for your friendship, dedication, and leadership.

Mike Starich and Tim Isacco, your leadership at Orion is simply A+. I could not be more proud of two people. Thank you for continuing to build the Orion legacy and for your support of our veterans—you are both priceless.

LJ Hirnikel, my great friend and Orion and NSTAR business partner, you are the most dedicated worker I have ever met in my life and our success was directly attributed to your tireless efforts. Without you, we simply wouldn't have achieved so much—not even close. "I" means "we" in this book.

Darrell McDaniel, thank you for being a great friend and for stepping into the leadership role at a critical juncture in NSTAR's global expansion. I am anxious to see the next chapter and know with your leadership, the sky is the limit!

To the employees of Orion and NSTAR, I want to say that I'm proud to have been associated with each of you; your passion and commitment to our vision are to be commended and respected. My hope is that we have helped you and your families build your own lives in positive ways, the same way you have helped build Orion and NSTAR. Every bit of our success has your fingerprints on them. THANK YOU.

Lou Pollock, in Navy ROTC at Miami, you taught me that leadership came in many different forms and in different types of people. You believed in me and that catapulted me to success in my own life; I would not be the person I am today without your guidance and support.

Ellen Wojahn, where do I start? *The Second Decision* was a team effort and I am proud to serve alongside you in getting this book out to entrepreneurs; your work is second to none. Thank you for helping me to tell the story that people would want to read, not just what I would want to write.

Advantage Media, my publisher, I am amazed at what you do and grateful for every person I have had the pleasure to work with—what a great success story you are now writing for your own company, it's truly impressive.

Verne Harnish, you are my mentor and my entrepreneurial role model. You started EO and today it has over 10,000 members. You started Gazelles and today it helps thousands of businesses align and reach their true potential. You changed my life at BOG. Thank you, I would not be half the entrepreneur I am if I had not had the fortune of meeting you 15 years ago.

To all of you in the Entrepreneur Organization (EO) and EO Entourage and Rogue Forums, thank you for all of your invaluable input over the past few years, including naming the book! Thank you to Jim Baker and Mike Malone for co-founding the Raleigh chapter of EO and for every leader who has continued to build it since 1998. This was a life changer and game changer for the business. For all of my friends in EO, I value your friendship and your business knowledge; I am thankful to spend time with people much smarter than myself that constantly raise the bar.

To all of you in Vistage, my other CEO peer group, thank you for the same constant support and input over the past four years, starting with that dreadful presentation that led to me writing this book! Ten years with each of you has been one of the most impactful phases of my entire life. We talk about our personal and family journeys while we learn about business from fantastic speakers and our fellow members…I'm looking forward to the next ten. Thank you Bill Buxton for leading such an impactful group, you are without peers!

To all of you at the Shelton Leadership Center and to its founder, General H. Hugh Shelton, I am honored to have served alongside each and every one of you for the last 12 years. You are truly incredible people who have made measurable improvements to our society.

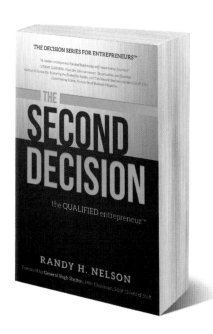

How can you use this book?

MOTIVATE

EDUCATE

THANK

INSPIRE

PROMOTE

CONNECT

Why have a custom version of *The Second Decision?*

- Build personal bonds with customers, prospects, employees, donors, and key constituencies

- Develop a long-lasting reminder of your event, milestone, or celebration

- Provide a keepsake that inspires change in behavior and change in lives

- Deliver the ultimate "thank you" gift that remains on coffee tables and bookshelves

- Generate the "wow" factor

Books are thoughtful gifts that provide a genuine sentiment that other promotional items cannot express. They promote employee discussions and interaction, reinforce an event's meaning or location, and they make a lasting impression. Use your book to say "Thank You" and show people that you care.

The Second Decision is available in bulk quantities and in customized versions at special discounts for corporate, institutional, and educational purposes. To learn more please contact our Special Sales team at:

1.866.775.1696 • sales@advantageww.com • www.AdvantageSpecialSales.com